A Reason 2 Cry

By

Carlos V. Bellamy

ISBN: 1-4033-9260-9 (e-book)
ISBN: 1-4033-9261-7 (Paperback)

Library of Congress Control Number: 2002095573

This book is printed on acid free paper.

Printed in the United States of America
Bloomington, IN

1stBooks – rev. 11/22/02

Contents

Prologue

Everybody has a reason to cry. I figured if I gave you mine maybe you could relate to my trials and tribulations. I've endured a lot of hardships within my short lifespan. But crying was unheard of. It was for wimps and cry babies. Especially being that the streets raised me. To get caught crying was to get caught showing weakness. And the streets devoured those who showed weakness.

Now, don't take my words out of context. When I speak about crying I'm not specifically talking about a physical tear. Just like there are plenty of reasons to cry, there are plenty of ways to cry. Stress builds up and it demands to be relieved. You can't keep things bottled-up. Its plain unhealthy to do so. Growing up on the streets I had valid reasons to cry. Just never did.

Being that I've matured, I'd like the opportunity to cry. Whatever my reason may be for crying, I feel I should take the time to cry. With that in mind, this book is my heart. These pages are my eyes. These words are my tears. Who says a man aint suppose to cry?

Like I said, everybody has a reason to cry. But everybody don't cry.

I. CAPTURED EMOTIONS

We all have pain, some just greater than others.
"L.O.S"

A Poem For Mom
to: my mother Sharon

A rose is still a rose. As time passes my love for you only grows.
The wind blows thoughts of beauty…the beauty of a mother and child.
Let us pray for awhile, then let us walk a mile. Do smile.
As we walk through hardships, let us remember yesterdays' memories.
As we walk through tribulations, let us remember todays' messages.
As we walk through the gates of hope, let us remember tomorrows'
promises.
One step at a time is the best way to go through this storm.
You are unforgettable by birth and I'm proud to be your first born.
The days of August are precious to me for eternity.
Those days brought forth the woman who gave birth to me.
From the depths of my heart I would like to take the time to say
that until the next one, I wish this to be your happiest birthday!

L.O.S.

Love is...

dedicated to my loving grandmother
a childhood memory forever alive

Love is...a reunion of family reminiscing on both good and
bad times.

Love is...a greeting card, sent with the intentions to uplift
a lonely spirit.

Love is...warm words, which can be a raincoat to repel the
relentless rain.

Love is...the emotions of a mother who has a passion for
nurturing her offspring.

Love is...a grandmother who passes on wisdom as a tool to
enlighten her youth.

Love is...a relationship between friends built on truth and
honesty.

Love is...a bond that can never be broken.

Love is...the memory of yesterday. The essence of today.
The expectations of tomorrow.

Love is...eternal.

Love is...forever.

Love is...You!

L.O.S.

Carlos Bellamy

<u>Remain True</u>
dedicated to Crystal
hopefully this will inspire you to correspond

I know its hard for you to picture me like this.
Behind bars treated like a misfit.
My lifestory an example of how hard it gets
Listen up Crys, no matter what happens you'll always be my lil sis.
You might not know what to say, you might feel shame.
If you live for yesterday, we'll never eliminate the pain.
I offer you a challenge, express your words through poetry.
If you accept, then use your poetry.
We'll talk through poetry and we'll discuss any topic you choose.
That way we'll be able to relate to how it is in each others' shoes.
My love for family especially including you
will always remain true.

L.O.S.

Smile For Me
to: my cousin Leon

Growing up was rough, it seems we never had enough.
Fighting against the odds, my God—we really did have it tough.
Even though we have disputed sometimes, all is fine.
Even though we have committed crimes, fighting as if drunk and blind.
The love of cousins never fade, it only strengthens with time.
If we count the wrongs we've done each other, we'll count until the sun set.
There's very few moments that we shared that I deeply regret.
As of yet, I'm willing to bet—that even when we were hostile
We took the time to smile. If you remember 'G', then smile for me.
What happened to the days of old, the days when we were full of laughs?
Life has sent us down separate, but weary paths.
Talented in so many ways, I've stumbled in a maze—there's only one way
out.
If I die, don't cry. Say your goodbye and remember what I was about.
If there's a paradise for a soldier,
I pray Jehovah bless me. Someway. Somehow.
May I rest in peace in my loved ones memory, smile for me now.

L.O.S.

If
to: my friend Tashaun

If you take a look into my eyes you'll see pure surprise.
I didn't expect you to stick around, but you did when all the rest left.
You've kept me alive in your memories with each thought and every breath.
What did I do to deserve your attention, but be a friend.
If all is as you claim, if our love is true then I pray it will never end.
When all else fails I shall hold on to hope—as I requested.
As long as you remain close I hold no grudges against being tested.
Through it all only faith can allow us to escape the claws of hate.
My eyes glisten as I listen to words delivered from the heart.
Pride will not allow me to shed tears for all the years we've been apart.
But on the inside I cry. Yes I cry because I feel the pains of a ghost.
Remember me always. Your loving friend, A.K.A dat nigga Los.

L.O.S.

<u>In Memory Of The Past</u>
to: my friend Crystal

Unforgettable moments stenciled into my heart
The thrills of being a part, of something new—something different.
A close relationship between friends, once beautiful and elegant.
By sharing secrets a bond blossomed over the years.
Laughs and memorable instances, smiles and heart-broken tears.
When the burden upon your shoulders became an unbearable load
I kept you company as you traveled down a dark and dreary road.
You confided in me. Trusted me with your thoughts.
And I done the same.
Now you're like a ship that passes by
as I struggle to remember her name.
Our wills were strong, but time proved to be stronger.
Our memories were long, but distance proved to be longer.
Life goes on…people tends to forget
What was once a beautiful friendship, now struggles just to exist.
Remember me, through the good times and the misery
For when you need a ear to hear
the excitable and the news that you fear
…I will always be hear. Always and forever.
Now ya feel me?

L.O.S.

Carlos Bellamy

Pieces Of A Man
to: Big Red's wife

As I look upon my past, my heart shatters like glass.
Pieces fall everywhere and the only ones who can pick
them up are those that care.

Surviving as one is hard, believe me I understand.
But life is hectic when trying to survive as pieces of a man.
I will never be whole again as long as we are apart.
Valuing your letters as I received them, cherishing words from the heart.
You say you remember, do you remember me sincerely?
You name special events, but fail to remember me vividly.
True love never dies, it can always be renewed.
Happiness can be found again and old vows can be reused.
Til death do us part, betrayed by confusion.
Its hard to believe, impossible to conceive—you hint our love is an illusion.
You consider yourself as one, but pieces of me have been instilled within.
Leave me if you must, but let it be known I'll never love again.
For better or worse, through sickness and health, for richer or poor
…but now you claim our love is nevermore.
At least you could pick up the pieces…
…She left them on the floor.

L.O.S.

<u>Our Love</u>
to: old man Will's girl

Our love embraces my soul and takes me to a special place.
In my dreams I often chase your smiling face.
I lay in my bed and reminisce for awhile.
I often recall the sweet taste of your lips and your sexy smile.
Chinese food for two on Taylor street.
Quiet walks at night along the beach.
It is these things that fills my heart.
It is these things that also tears me apart.
Separated for too long. All I ask
is for you to be strong until I come home.
Captivated and hypnotized by your sensuous brown eyes.
The pleasure of our love lies in between your thighs.
Enchanted by your exotic essence it's the presence
of your fragrance that fills my nostrils with enticing smells.
God bless the day lil Will was born.
What a precious moment. Do tell.
Loving you. Holding you. Caressing you. Squeezing you.
For better or worse, our love remains true.

L.O.S.

<u>Always</u>
to: Sharonda, my beloved daughter
I have always been there.
I will always be there.
(Meo)

Envision a father with a daughter he truly loves.
If ever separated, the tears of doves
instantly unleashed from above.
Sharonda, I have always been there.
My love fully expressed by the arcanes of air.
Forget me as I am now, remember me by our last embrace.
Before my world transformed into an abyss of hate.
Journey with me as I travel within.
Picturing your brown eyes, long hair and skin.
Collect calls and letters of love keeps you within.
Reasons for me to struggle on and grin.
Pieces of me instilled within you and Tyrone.
Remember me always. My heart is your home.
Even after I'm physically gone
I'll always be there. You will never be alone.
You pierced the interior of my soul.
Make me say it again girl.
You pierced the interior of my soul.
Need I say it again girl?
In my own words "before you, never knew
what joy was. You became the world to me.
Always."

L.O.S.

Destined To Be
writtten for my cellmate Storm
dedicated to his soulmate

We met coincidentally at Gala Lane.
You belonged to another, but your heart wanted change.
81/2—critics claim love never endures.
81/2—critics never had a love so pure.
Spiritual, emotionally sweet and fiesty.
Highly sensitive and humble—you completely excite me.
At times life is a paradox, complex and untrue.
In this pit of hate, where darkness is more than a state
My thirst for light is quenched when I dwell on you.
Promise to always remain friends with you.
Do whatever it takes for you
To make life happy for you.
Even if I have to compromise myself for you.
Shocked and overwhelmed when Jaide appeared.
Your innocence, my joy that's what she bared.
Aries and Pisces, the alpha and omega of life.
Prophecies yearning to be filled. Thoughts of a husband and wife.
I have matured behind bars.
You matured behind bars.
Amber stones and Jaide gems.
Destined to be.
Soulmates inseparable from within.
Destined to be.
My heart an oracle of our love.
Destined to be.

L.O.S.

<u>Expressions Of Our Love</u>
to: Dan—dedicated for wifey(Delores)

Expressions of our love
are numerous and definitely sent from above.
Seventeen years since we first met.
The most memorable was when you said "I accept."
Envision us as we journey to the museum of Science and Industry.
From there the Chicago Theatre.
From there the Sybaris, sensual ectasy.
Expressions of our love.
I'll try anything! Ask Taste of Honey.
I'll try anything! Ask Smokey Robison.
Expressions of our love.
Compassionate as you are you mean the world.
Real sweet and caring you're my kind of girl.
Words do me no justice, they only limit my love.
Derrick, Delorian, Darmika…
…expressions of our love.

L.O.S.

A Bike Ride
to: **Lenard Clark, dedication**

A racial spark was lit
and Lenard Clark was hit
Beat-down in the streets of Bridgeview
bloody body stretched-out for all to view

To 35th let us ride!
All he wanted was a bike ride
To 35th let us travel!
The strength of the blacks will unravel

In the hospital torn apart
is where the stars came to see Clark
Mary J. dropped by
Jesse comforted his mother when she started to cry

To 35th let us ride!
All he wanted was a bike ride
To 35th let us travel!
The strength of the blacks will unravel

Turn on the news, let us hear about that black boy
The one that was whooped by three white boys
They really gone go to jail fo that?
I dun seen it all and thats a fact

Is that Mrs. Clark on the news
Sayin forgive that white boy fo what he did do?
I dun seen it all, now aint that something?
She must be getting paid or somethin!

L.O.S.

13

<u>Your Last Breath</u>
dedicated to Tupac Amaru Shakur
as you grew, I grew
still I rise, still you rise, still we rise

I have listened to your lyrics and read your poetry.
Our inner thoughts similar, for we both stumbled unknowingly.
A love unspoken, yet my heart heard it well.
The promise of dreams broken, the truth forever hidden in a shell.
Destiny's definition of a concrete rider with ambition.
The hurt intense as I write this elaborate composition.
A rose grew, blossoming despite heartaches and pain.
Only to be torn apart by winter winds and worldly rain.
Even now, I can feel the after effects of that treacherous hurricane.
Sometimes I cry without shedding a physical tear.
If there's pain…then Afeni my dear
We'll embrace that which the imprudent fear.
In my mind we stroll down memory lane.
We met at Brenda's house.
Remember…after the baby drove her insane.
Nuttin 2 Lose, you were trapped inside a Violent Soljah Story.
As Life Goes On, it seems to suffer is mandatory.
I screamed "No More Pain!" Lord Knows society ignored me.
I miss you Pac.
How can I miss you, when its as if you never left?
As far as your death
my heart refuses to accept the notion of your last breath.
It Aint Easy…eloquently put.

L.O.S.

14

II. The Depths Of Darkness

To be enlightened is to be awakened from a deep sleep.
"L.O.S"

The Hearts Of Men

The embrace of evil is like the memory of a forgotten lover—it takes you by
surprise.
Yesterdays runaway. Todays die inorder for tomorrows to be born.
Hope lingers in the air, battling with legions of despair.
The silence of the graves screams curses to the living.
It is the deepness of this silence, that feels mankind with dread.
Slaves of fear, the bravest must struggle to be brave.
Is it death, or the simplicity of life in which we are afraid?
Is our purpose to solve every unanswered question?
Why must trials and tribulations be the equivalence of hard-earned lessons?
Throw me in the dungeons of the world if you must.
I will betray my heart and imprison myself within my mind.
The ways of this wicked world are like the rays of a false pearl.
The hearts of saints is like sunshine,
While evil rejoices in the moonlight.
I declare the laws of society unjust.
Judge me not Sons of Satan!
I disown the flesh, substitute it with the blood of the lamb.
Oh! Ye unfaithful be grateful, that you have been spared his wrath.
Life can only be what it is and nothing more.

L.O.S.

Pools of Blood

An aborted soul, Society chose to exercise pro-choice.
My voice hoarse from hollering "light the torch!"
Dead but still breathing
the theft of my free will has left me bleeding.
Overwhelmed by urban grief
the poverty of the streets is unique
in the sense aint no love when trapped underneath.
Penitentiaries and public aid.
Fatal diseases both man-made.
The hypocrisy of an American democracy has us slowly dying.
A testament of courage will be revealed in due time.
Broken homes with cracked windows and unlocked doors.
Silent weapons is issuing quiet wars.
Populations controlled. Prophecies untold.
In this day and age the mistakes and aches of old continuously unfold.
Talk no more! Let us challenge the depth of death.
Celestial lights desperately waiting for us to accept.
Painful premonitions of our mothers after they wept.
The penalty of death should be left for God to judge.
Who will rise before we all die unloved?
Let us embrace destiny and walk through Pools of Blood.

L.O.S.

<u>Titus</u>

The windows to the past have been closed.
Regret and shame, I see them no more.
My deeds although treacherous and immoral
I see them no more.
Who but dares to mutter a syllable of unrest?
Let us ignore the accusations and the blasphemy of the unjust?
My woes visualized and yet unseen.
My cries heard and not an ear registered my silent screams.
Not a soul stirred, for society deemed
I was nothing more than a sorry pitiful thing.
Unpleasant here and nows, and wretched yesterdays.
What is this!?!?! Bright lights devoid of shade!
With a ghost gaze, I can see where dead antelope's graze.
Was my time on this dreaded Earth
nothing more than a relentless curse?
Listen! Can you hear the shadows of uneased souls
whispering from the depths of the hearse?
Well, I do and I don't. I can and I won't!
Mirrors with no reflections. Souls deprived of affection!
My heart a corpse in a tomb, awaiting resurrection.

L.O.S.

Subliminal Messages

Concentration camps, no different from modern day prisons.
Chary chasms charity for the chaste of hearts.
Rehabilitation? I've heard the concept, but what is it?
Its unfamiliar to me. Can Society explain it please?
This punitive system has considerably damaged me.
Impaired in the cerebral and yet enhanced in the cerebral.
Mindstates altered, desperately switched to cope with pain.
Subliminal messages once uncanny and strange
suddenly necessary to maintain.
"They can incarcerate my body, but my mind will be free!"
I hear you, but how long will it last?
"They've incarcerated me and it seems I'll never be free!"
Guess it didn't last.
It never lasts.
Gimics. Unfamiliar tactics instantaneously allies.
What was once silly and absurd, we now use to pass days by.
Steel bars, brick walls-different shades of gray.
Journey where misery is accompanied by decay.
Where illusions whisper the names of grief and disarray.
Where churchgoers and frequent worshippers are led astray.
Where God is a myth that diminishes with each day.
Subliminal Messages.

L.O.S.

III. PRIME POETRY

Love does not hurt. Once it does its no longer love
Its attachment.
"J-'_ '-Bone"

<u>Remember Me?</u>
to: Nicole, my first and only true love

it is said often that love don't last, but if strong enough it can be renewed.
happiness can be found again and old vows can be reused. Remember me.

Remember me? better yet, the day we met. The events are still unclear.
Did I wink or simply blink, or was it God's grace that brought you near?
Walk with me. Take a look—into the life of a labeled crook.
My pain runs deep. At night I lie awake, while my body screams for sleep.
Everyday I pray Jehovah will release the pain.
Since the day we abandoned each other, my life's never been the same.
Remember me?
Isley Brothers at my house. The sweet taste of your enticing mouth.
Its not hard to tell, you were waiting to exhale—you could've let it out.
Victoria Secrets…the best threads for a female to wear.
Picture me bare, except for teddy bear underwear.
Living for the love of you. Sex in the rain—unfulfilled fantasies.
When you walked out of my life, my soul wailed and my heart dropped—
down on bending knees.
For a love as strong as ours to have lasted, what did it take?
Certainly not uncorrected mistakes, uneased heart breaks, or unfelt aches.
Remember me?
I hear your heart-melting smile has been passed to a child—do maintain.
I hope indeed, God bless your seed—Naudia, what a beautiful name.
If I die, will you cry? Will our love be remembered as true or a lie?
Things once cherished, easily perish when put to test.
Til my dying days my love will wander without a place to rest.
Remember me?

L.O.S.

<u>Never Will</u>
Nicole's perspective

I'm writing this piece to let you know
although we're more than friends its time for me to go.
No longer can I listen to your pain.
Another month of your misery and I'll be insane.
Carlos, I want you to know that I tried hard
but to love you is to hate God.
These are my true feelings, forgive me if they're harsh or cruel.
I ask you to forget our love, as I will soon forget you.
On the phone when we discussed our future and fate
I said if one of us was incarcerated the other shouldn't wait.
I've moved to another state and I'm married with two kids.
I'm happy and content with the life I live.
I was never in love. I was infatuated with the idea.
When you read this, together we'll release a tear.
These are all the words I never wrote.
These are all the words I never spoke.
I never got to tell you how I feel.
I never got the chance to stay true and be real.
Now that I think about it dear,
I never wrote what you see here.
What you see here is everything you wanted to hear
but never will...
...wake up! You're dreaming.

L.O.S.

In Honor Of A Lost Love
the forbidden sonnet

My heart can not give birth to a new love.
Instead it holds on to old flames with a desperate grip.
My heart can not know another love.
Instead into pits of sorrow and remorse I slip.
Love intensifies, falling in love with itself.
Enchanted with desire, the destiny of constellations unfold.
In the beginning she filled my heart with pleasure;
in the end she emptied the joy from within my soul.
Love disappears, illusions of its former self.
Stumbling down an unknown path searching for assurance.
My passion is too immense. My quest for fulfillment incomplete.
Betrayed by bewilderment, my loves' cousin—confusion;
her mistress name is pretense.
In my twisted mouth misery is far from bitter and revenge tastes sweet.
When I sleep I can hear my love. Her voice is extremely faint.
Renewal is understanding, therefore my love is lost and I shall remain blank.

L.O.S.

The Heartbeat Of A Heart
**dedicated to those who've been
torn between two loves**

My love, my tree of life—reasons for me to continue in an ungodly world.
She illuminates my aura, forcing me to abandon the darkness.
I can not know another love, because my love is the ultimate love.
Heavenly is her essence, blessed is the foundations of her testament.
The forbidden sonnet—dedicated to the memory of young love.
As time passes my thoughts begin to wander.
My heart betrays me. My eyes, a transgression upon my humble soul.
How can I look at another woman with unpure thoughts?
How can I dare try to replace the beauty of that which I lost?
Can I tell her?
SHUT YOUR MOUTH!!!
Should I tell her?
SHUT YOUR MOUTH!!!
My love does not remember me. She has moved on, she knows me not.
BLASPHEMY! WHY UTTER SUCH VILE THOUGHTS???
WHY CORRUPT MY EARS WITH THE ADULTERATE PLAGUE
YOU'VE CAUGHT???
Can I confide in her?
SHE WILL NOT UNDERSTAND!!!
Who whispers to me with a voice so resonant?
Its as if they possess the identity of my past.
Who is it that dares to speak?
Who can be so bold as to torment the crumbled walls where my heart
sleeps?
IT IS I. HEAR THE HEARTBEAT OF A HEART.
IT IS I. HEAR THE HEARTBEAT OF A HEART.

L.O.S.

Declaration Of Love

Who am I?

I am deeply in love, ecstasy embraces me.
My heart has been filled with affinity.
To be fond of, devoted to, to feel warm towards her.
That is what makes me love loving her.

We met on a Sunday. She was my elder by ten years.
When life hurt her and brought her to tears
it was I she cuddled. It was I.
Misery instantly relieved. It was I.

Although my kindred is not known for having sense
I am not average my passion is immense.
I feel. I love. I grow as time continues.
The welfare of my love is my only menu.

We met on a Sunday. She was my elder by ten years.
When life hurt her and brought her to tears
It was I she cuddled. It was I.
Misery instantly relieved. It was I.

They say we are not to be together.
I defy conventialism. We shall be together.
Overcoming obstacles inorder to endure.
My love for my love is loyal and pure.

We met on a Sunday. She was my elder by ten years.
When life hurt her and brought her to tears
It was I she cuddled! It was I!
When she got married, where was I?
Declaration of love. Who am I?

L.O.S.

25

Carlos Bellamy

Alyson's Flute

Alyson, a sight to behold. A spectacle to be displayed.
Beauty for the eyes as well as for the ears.
I smile as she puts a flute to her sweet lips.
The sounds that ensued were sensual and ecstatic.
Music pleasant enough to entice a connoisseur.
Ears obsessed with enchanted melodies.
I watch as she performs a song for the libido.
Intimate in her own way she is the perfection of an artist.
Bewitched by slices of an american pie
I continue to watch fanatically.
She trembles, shivering as the sound she searched for
is brought forth into creation by the wielding of a fiery flute.

L.O.S.

IV. HEARTFELT HORROR

don't shed a tear, cuz momma I aint happy here.
after trial no mo smiles for a couple years.
"2-Pac"

Ghostly Painz

i am a prisoner within myself
tortured by my very existence

Time flies, but where does it go?
That is something numerous would like to know.
Why live when eventually we must die?
What good is laughter, knowing one day soon you'll cry?
These are our Ghostly Painz.

Mother, don't you dare weep!
For me—please rest your weary soul with comfort and sleep.
You are not at fault. It is I who must wear the blame.
For me—please shed your coat of sorrow and your hat of shame.
These are your Ghostly Painz

Dead but still breathing. Scarred by unwise choices.
I am haunted by the spirits of the wind and their accusing voices.
I have laid down my cloak of pretense, for the agony's immense.
Lord knows, my heart desires peace and a need to be content.
These are my Ghostly Painz.

L.O.S.

I Give you My Pain

an intimate view into an exquisite heart
meant for debonair eyes to see

I give you my pain. My façade is unmasked
and my shields are lowered.
My heart stands naked and exposed in front of you.
I give you my pain, inorder to strengthen you.

Deprived as a child, poverty was a constant companion.
I ran the streets with hunger and bathed with discontent.
Three-deep in a bathtub
eight bodies in a two bedroom apartment.
I give you my pain, because the burden is too heavy to bare.

It was written for me to succeed
ambushed by greed I was deceived to fail.
I stole to feed my thirst.
Hunger forced me to accept a life of hustling and dirt.
False highs and phantom promises destined to be my curse.
I give you my pain, can you relate to how I hurt?

As I wander aimlessly through the forest
I'm saddened to see a fire in the woods.
Separated from familiarities, I unknowingly search for solitude.
Overwhelmed with hate, I suppress all feelings.
My love lies dormant, a sleeping beauty.
I give you my pain, now what will you do?

I give you my pain, because I care for you.

L.O.S.

All That I Am

All that I am is an island of hope, surrounded by a lake of misery.
Shackled in chains, who can I blame but me for my repulsive history.
A reflection of the past that has been molded into shape.
I pray Jehovah release the tremendous weight.
Is it possible that I shall be remembered upon death?
All that I am is a corpse that has been granted breath.
Dead on the inside, is it too late to realize
understanding is considered a prize?
A blessing can be a curse and a curse a blessing in disguise.
But I shall take shelter in hope and cast misery into that fiery lake.
Only faith can eliminate the fact that my heart harbors hate.
All that I am is a walking flame
that has been engulfed with intense pain.
If it is true that I have disgraced my familys' name
Then upon my cloak of iniquity
I shall allow you to stitch buttons of shame.
I shall not hold my head down long. For when my pain is gone
then and only then shall tomorrow bring thoughts of a rejoiceful song.
In debt to family and true friends, because they have guided me
to sing a song that will eventually set my soul free.
All that I am is a continuation of all that I was born to be.

L.O.S.

The Promise Of Life

Remember me, is all I ask. Recognize my name.
Is their hope, or are we to be victimized by our ghostly pains?
Through it all the hearts of men introduces us to sin.
Reflections of the past, at last subtle thoughts of making amends.
Picture a pack of mortal peers petrified with prison years.
When approached with the shadows of night, daylight runs.
Ease my soul with street rhymes if hard times come.
Why contemplate about death, or be obsessed with thoughts of living long?
If only I had a son, reasons for a legacy to carry on.
Although my heart is torn, filled with sarcasm and scorn
As long as your heart shall remain warm,
then my heart shall remain warm.
Like whispering winds friends come and leave.
But it is true friends that shine in times of need.
Be not deceived, the Earth bleeds and the skies cry.
Heaven clashes with the fury of Hell before my very eye.
Turning the promise of life into a curse,
for the hearse is not for us to deny.

L.O.S.

Carlos Bellamy

Through It All
**"And how do we punish those whose remorse
is already greater than their misdeed?"
'Unknown'**

No one saw my pain, no one cared to look.
But they dared, to stare at a classified crook.
To them I was just another bad chapter in life's book.
How can I die? Knowing I'll never effect those who I tried to seek.
How can I die? Knowing only Mother and few others will weep.
Bottle-up my misery and sell it two for ten.
Living in the mist of sin. My life…My life in the pen.
How long must I suffer? 50? 20? hopefully no more than ten.
Some say pray everyday and the pain will run away.
Others claim there's no pain, and act as if its not there.
But their eyes betray them and I realize deep down they care.
My heart aches and is hurting, my soul is weighed down with the burden
of penitentiary years. A lifetime of tears for dead peers.
In the end, I almost bend, when the madness overwhelms the cheers.
I am not sure, but in my dreams it seems the only Kure
is to die hard, while remaining faithful and pure.
Will I fail or will I prevail? Backed against a wall, I must not fall.
Subdued to a crawl. I will stand next to Jehovah through it all.

L.O.S.

Incarcerated Ills

If only I would've known…maybe things would've been different.
Irrelevant desires to be elegant. Hallucinations of a clairvoyant.
The repercussions of sin harmonizes the consequences of chasing cream.
If life was a dream, would you want to wake up?
If you sold your soul to Satan and he cheated, would you try to break up?
If only I would've known…If what I know now I knew then.
Unforgotten days brings us a birth of cursed breaths.
With a conflicted heart I embrace a soldiers death.
My life secrets exposed, revealed, and unkept!
Mother wept, for she only knew my surface.
If only I would've known…If what I know now I knew then.
On this dreaded night I envision the struggle of my ancestors' plight.
The forever fight for freedom.
My only fear is the future of our children. Who will lead them?
Will they be harshly affected by that which we arrogantly neglected?
It is to be expected for the dead to bury their own.
If only I would've known…If what I know now I knew then.
Inspired with hopes of Heaven and fears of a fiery Hell.
Confined to a prison cell, penitentiary pain prevails.
I offer all who read this, to enter into the abyss through me.
For in this mist, tomorrow's sorrows
can not be overwhelmed by the eternity of yesterdays agony.

L.O.S.

Carlos Bellamy

<u>A Testament Of Courage</u>
In memory of a century; my 24 years of pain

To defile the purpose of living
is to destroy that which was given.
Sufficient treasures lay hidden
invisible to the common eye.
Must we die to live or do we live to die?

On this paper I capture my soul
and to he who remembers me I give control.
Immortal portraits, reflections of a spiritual mirror.
The shadows of death creeps, continuously drawing nearer.
The elusive essence of life is yet to become clearer.

Imagine nature with amnesia in the year two.
Picture the sun with alzheimers, cold becomes cruel.
My will a testament of courage. I bequeath it to you.
If in the morning we shall meet with a sudden and predictable end
then tonight I shall smile for I never knew a true friend.

L.O.S.

<u>The Challenge Stands</u>

I've realized I don't want to die.
Not without accomplishing my goals.
I've realized I sought death as a means to escape.
I've challenged both God and Satan.
My words belligerent and blatant.

I've realized I don't want to die.
Not without seeing what the future holds.
Its not that I'm scared to die now.
Don't want to be punished for a precarious past.
Not while smelling the promise of hope!
Not while tasting the joy of diligence!
Not while hearing the echoes of my own talent!

I've realized I don't want to die.
I want to elevate and excel.
Inhale what I feel and think.
Sink into the depths of my mind
and embrace that which makes me shine.

I've realized I don't want to die
but the challenge stands.

L.O.S.

Carlos Bellamy

How About A Third?

In life we make mistakes, the repercussions sincerely severe.
When startled by earthquakes, the outcome isn't always clear.
Second chances arrive and must be held dear.
How about a third?

I often imagine myself back home, after my first X.
Living devoid of stress
heart harboring aspirations, only legends caress.
But destiny being complex and untrue
has twisted my fate and left me without what I was due.
Jehovah I hear second chances come from you.
How about a third?
As a child it seemed, I was constantly under quarantine.
If I wanted to place blame, I could name a father unseen.
A mother with secrets, a squad of siblings who stole personal things.
Jehovah I hear second chances are for those redeemed.
How about a third?
As I sit confined in a bleak cell.
I often wonder if this prison pain will prevail.
Mortal prayers aimed for Heaven, desperately dismissing Hell.
Jehovah I hear second chances are for fairy tales.
But I attest to being living proof, my second chance has failed.
How about a third?

L.O.S.

V. KEYS OF LIFE

You will be a long way from home, unless home is your
Ability to persevere and overcome.
"Unknown"

Carlos Bellamy

<u>Stanzas Of The Collected Variety</u>

Sometimes hard work hurts.
It is then that we need the strength of the church.
Inorder to sustain a heavenly mindstate
trust and faith in the Lord is what it takes.
To: Aunt Leola

At times it seems that dreams fade away.
Love dissolves into illusions. Reflections of a brighter day.
Whisper his name and he shall scream yours.
For it is a wonderful Lord that opens heavenly doors.
To: Cousin Tameka

Although reality may be vicious
close your eyes and embrace vivid pictures
of passionate premonitions.
Yesterday's tomorrow is indeed here.
Holding on to the threads of hope, we have nothing to fear.
To: Sharon, my mother

L.O.S.

Haiku—Assorted Collections

The Armor Of The Heart

Let not the armor

of the heart be easily

pierced by deadly words.

A Living Nightmare

Yesterdays mornings

are here and today is still

a living nightmare.

Surrounded

All I am is an

island of hope surrounded

by misery's lake.

Live And Learn

What you forget to

remember is based on you

live and learn, start new.

L.O.S.

Carlos Bellamy

Respect Ourselves
this is dedicated to the ignorant
those who blame others for their predicaments—respect ourselves!

Remember me? Recognize my name. I have cost my love ones plenty pain.
Eyes full of tears. Is it too late to change? If it is, I must try anyway.
Searching for a brighter day, I've been led astray.
Please! If you feel my pain take the time to pray.
Even though I have sinned, I have tried to make amends.
Can I be true to the ghetto, while maintaining my spiritual friend?
Thinking about all my deeds, of my unborn seeds.
Will they be tangled by these wicked weeds?
Of all the things I've done, remorse I have never felt. That's true.
Under a ghetto I've been laid—so I shed a tear or two.
Remember me? Recognize my name. Jehovah witness my pain.
Sorrow, pain and agony. Born a bastard into a life of misery.
Eventually my life will cease, but before my time comes I hope I find peace.
Live and let die. Bury me high, then wipe the tears from my Mother's eye.
Vicious! Malicious! The cruel world we know. The ghetto.
Emotions. We must place them on life's shelves.
Silence! To my fellow brothers, we must struggle to respect ourselves.

L.O.S.

<u>Is Their Hope</u>

I chose a way of life, a way you say is not good.
Society says I'm wrong, but I claim I'm simply misunderstood.
label me violent, a thug—because of my nature I'm not right.
Tell me! Who are you to harass me, due to my style of life?
Hardships—I've seen face to face. Discrimination—I've had my taste.
Erase racism! Take a look into the abyss, the pits of our very soul.
Incarcerate our bodies, but beware! our minds maintain control.
Release the pain, shackled in chains—it runs deep.
bury me high in the sky. aint that where they lay a good guy?
Hope—we search for daily, but we can not find.
oppressed and deemed crazy, but we can not stay blind.
Power? For it we die. Freedom? we try, but society lie.
Even thugs cry. Is their hope???

L.O.S.

Suicide: Hear My Cry For Help

a prisoner's escape

Hand me a sheet
and let me dangle by the bars.
Things have gotten too deep
all I have left is prison scars.

My ears full of noise. "Guard! Guard!"
"If you can't do the time don't do the crime!"
Hear my cry for help, suicide is so hard.
"That white boy was already dyin!"

My ears full of noise. Voices of inmates.
All I want to do is depart
now I'm surrounded by anger and hate.
They hold the same intentions as I close to heart.

A coward for trying. Brave for not doing it.
"Catwalk, put a bullet in his eye!"
Brave for trying. A coward for not doing it.
"That white boy aint want to die!"

Don't be scared to cry the road is close.
I write this cuz I feel his pain.
Unchain the physical, the spirit means the most.
I suffer on for those who chose not to remain.

L.O.S.

<u>Family</u>

This is a poem for family.
I dedicate this to those who try to understand me.
Intimate moments pass only to be missed.
As we reminisce we pray the future holds eternal bliss.
I send a kiss to you and wait for one to return.
You send a kiss to me. In our hearts is where our love burns.
A mother and two sisters.
I send a hug to you and wait for one to return.
You send a hug to me. In our hearts is where our love burns.
A father and three brothers.
I send a hug to me and wait for one to return.
I hug myself. In my heart is where my love burns.
A prodigal son.
It is your strength that strengthens me completely.
It is your love that holds me continuously.
It is your courage that allows me to walk courageously.
It is family.
This is a poem for family.

L.O.S.

Carlos Bellamy

I Defy Death

To be remembered, is that not the greatest gift?
Your memories of me makes me immortal.
I shall never die!
I will live on, powerful and strong!
A testament of excellence, an umbrella to life's storm.
Remember me and what I offered! Remember me and what I gave!
A birth of cursed breaths, embrace my mortal grave.
My hatred sustained. My love remains.
My misery, my confusions…let them be yours.
My quest for peace overwhelmed by Society's wars.
Forget me not. Allow me to be infinite in your memory.
I defy death!
Impregnate your seeds with my ghetto legacy.
I defy death!
Explicitly splendid, transcended forever.
Your memory is my fountain of youth—aint I clever?
I defy death!
As I stroll down the gardens of eternity forever.

L.O.S.

<u>It Hurts</u>
in answer to Dello's challenge of my potential

It hurts cuz the doors to the church are closed.
As I roam through the dark, I stumble through broken
glass and shattered windows.
Time passes and my hostility grows.
If I was to oppose the conventional ways of society
Will they expeditiously try and quiet me?
It hurts cuz I flirt with death daily.
How can I change when my past trails me?
My adversary is my future, to the cross it nails me.
As I walk through a forest of hatred, I simply stare.
Grotesque individuals fraudulently claim to be extraordinaire.
The façade and illusions of life is everywhere.
Let my lyrics be a religion to saints who thirst.
Let my virtues be a plague to Luciphers' curse.
If this is never to be, then this is why it hurts.

L.O.S.

Forget Me Never

The physical trap is easily invaded.
The mental snare once incurred becomes difficult to egress.
It is in my nature to reject sympathy.
The only way to help, is to extricate me from my pain.

A stranger and a friend encountered in the woods.
A reciprocal of each other
one is the reverse of the other
Let them journey towards enlightment.
Let them not be misguided or led astray
by the malicious opinions of the wayward animals.

I hunger for immortality.
My fountain of youth is found inside you.
My primary objective is to be remembered.
If you insist on helping, all I ask is
that you forget me never.

L.O.S.

If a Soldier Fall

Passionate premonitions of ungodly sins.
Shattered windows reveals that which lurks within.
The shuttle, concrete evidence that a journey had begun.
Now nothing more than a dream, one that never occurred.
What once was, what could have been
all different from what has transpired. The hearts of men
Sodom and Gomorrah—cities of sin.
Where unholy paths end, is where righteous ones end.
If we were given the chance to correct past mistakes
Would love be strong enough to eliminate the hate?
If I crippled myself, by giving you an arm and a leg
Would it be enough to help you fight what you dread?
The past can not be changed, but the future is waiting to be arranged.
From enemies to allies, isn't time strange?
I'll give my all if you give your all
Just be there if a soldier fall.

L.O.S.

Carlos Bellamy

The Sonnet Of The Mirror

I stare into the mirror. What I see I don't recognize.
As I stare into the mirror, what I see has left me horrified.
The bearer of truth Society's lies has left me ostracized.
Slipping into darkness, life's hard and my heart's petrified.
The mirror is cracked, so what I see is not purified.
My presence diminished, yet I reminisce about a hurricane.
As I reminisce about bliss, emotions instantly intensified.
My plight reversed! Now I grip the pain inorder to sustain.
My story written but unread, an inkling of a legend demanding to be heard.
A book of belligerent blames and aches, which arrogantly await.
No less than Malcom X, no greater than a bottle which lies on the curb.
Remember me always, forget me never. My epithet—the prodigy of hate.
The crack has been mended, the outcome has suddenly become clearer.
Embrace that which is portrayed in the sonnet of the mirror.

L.O.S.

<u>Why Do We?</u>

Why do we use words to hurt?
Why do we brutalize tender souls?
Why do we embrace profanity and welcome Adam's curse?
Why do we demand power and control?

Why do we lash out at the humble ones?
Why do we accept life at face value?
Why do we find comfort in the wrath of guns?
Why do we reject the complex as a virtue?

Why do we engulf peace with talons of hate?
Why do we search for truth, but accept lies?
Why do we wear masks, camouflaging character traits?
Why do we fear what is underneath, while doubting what's in the skies?

Why do we do what we do, knowing that what we do
is not what we are suppose to be aligned to.
"Loyal to you!"—my last words to I AM
…and his son too.

L.O.S.

Carlos Bellamy

<u>Untitled 1</u>

Slavery aint over it still exists.
Travel to the penitentiary and be a witness
to the entirety of life's hardships.
What you see will make you scream.
What you hear will make you cry.
To live and die, caged—devoid of hope
hands desperately gripping on to an abandoned dream.
Open your eyes! Uncover your ears!
Stand face to face—be subjected to our daily fears.
Beaten! Mistreated, punished cruel and unusually.
Brutality inflicted brutally, has become familiar
Its no longer new to me.
Blasphemously we measure our lifespan.
I know the Lord truly knows the hurt of this man.
So I await for biblical rain to come and cleanse the land.
A sinister soldier silently stumbling through segregated sand.
The laws of society are my chains.
The judicial system is a shackle upon my brain.
The courtroom has become my prison cell.
My soul searches for Heaven, while my body dwells in Hell.

L.O.S.

Untitled 2

The doors are shut. Sealed tight. They no longer revolve.
My heart an eternal riddle, one that even I am hard-pressed to solve.
An odyssey allegedly destined for the contour of the moon.
At last the shuttle has crashed, if any—survivors are doomed.
As time surpasses a profligate silhouette attempts
to stultify that which has become indefatigable.
A familiar friend named innocence, battered—bruised and rape.
Attacked by an unorthodox foreigner entitled hate.
My soul a contumacious candle to the maxims of society.
I embrace a prolific life underneath my shell of apathy.
The woods perfidious, the path diaphanous.
Reverse the curse, my thirst was never for birth.
The ignominy of the disillusioned is yet to be witnessed.
Arrogance, a foible that leads to tenuous business.
Let my words enlighten, follow the road to truth!
As I grow, my lessons of life I bequeath to you.
Take not offense! For it is the imprudent that do so.
If the same water runs down the river twice, we'll soon know.

L.O.S.

Carlos Bellamy

<u>Untitled 3</u>

Crippled! Forever incomplete. The limbs were not prosthetic.
In order to endure should I lace our hardships with antiseptic?
Can being overwhelmed with hate, possibly render me fake?
You speed as if in a race, you consume as if you have no taste.
I'll devour your words, only digesting what's prolific.
Forewarned of insidious behavior, but the omens were not specific.
Deliberate decisions to salvage what's been wrecked.
Its hard to swim through swamps of chaos and rivers of disrespect.
Your fall nothing but an illusion, you simply stumbled.
You saw me from afar, but I was close by—inside the jungle.
You make belligerent claims in regards to my departure,
I never left.
You make bold statements to reconcile what could be,
I sincerely accept.
Degrade you, me, us—nevermore shall I do such.
Our hearts actually combined and eternally touched.
You'll remember me, even if you say you won't.
You'll remember me, even if you say you can't.
You'll remember me, cuz to yourself I'll mold you to stay true.

L.O.S.

Untitled 4

You make inquiries that time will eventually reveal.
Question me how real, until prophecies are fulfilled.
Unaware of the snare, all I saw was celestial light.
Oblivious to malevolent manacles or minute plights.
Precise, my sentiments unconditional. You are respected.
Although redundant and superfluous, your every thought appreciated.
Even if I tried to live a lie
what you see in my eyes can never be disguised.
Let that which is perverse rest in a hearse
where it belongs.
It hurts to be cursed
yet we move on.
You inspire my lyrical fire. Uplift my natural gift.
Although you feel neglected, the notion is insane.
Random hearts accompanied by penitentiary pain.
Diligent and vigilant, security and fulfillment is yours to accept.

L.O.S.

Carlos Bellamy

ACKNOWLEDGEMENTS

I would like to acknowledge all who inspired me in the writing of my first book. First and foremost is my dearest mother Sharon. Love you Ma. Bryan, Alonzo, Deandre, Adrianne, and Crystal—my squad of siblings. Carl, the father who was there. Ward, the father who never knew me. Tupac Amaru Shakur, without you my skills wouldn't have elevated. Thug-life forever, dog. Gwendylon Brooks, rest your head. I couldn't have gotten over the hump without you! Dr. Margaret Burroughs, for being a friend when one was needed. To all those whose emotions I captured. To all those who captured my emotions. To all those who contributed in their own way. I love you all. Hopefully many more shall come. God bless.

Carlos Bellamy

Wherever The Wind Blows

Carlos Bellamy

Acknowledgements

I would like to acknowledge all who inspired me in the creation of my second poetry book. Highest praise goes to God. Without you there is no existence. To my family, love you all for yal support. Crutches needed to hold me up. Dr. Margaret Burroughs and Queen Mother, yal believed in me. To my creative writing class, for listening and pushing me forward. Can't forget Eric Drew. You kept me with something good to read. Inspiration comes in many forms. Rest in peace to Tupac Shakur, Juice, Uncle 'E', Big Bee, Ant, Grandma & Grandpa on my Daddy's side. Yal live on with my every breath. To every one whose life I have ever touched. To everyone who has ever touched my life. Love, plenty much. Oh yeah, 1-9 Kitchen big ups.

Carlos Bellamy

Contents

Preface

When I first started writing my inspiration to do so, was for the purposes of being remembered. After many talks with pundits and dilettantes, I've decided that many souls have been remembered. Some have been remembered for the wrong reasons, such as the wrongs they have inflicted. With that in mind being remembered is not as important to me. Memories are similar to history, in the sense that they both can be manipulated. As time goes on, what a person was once remembered for can change. My inspiration now is to touch lives. If you touch somebody's life they will always remember. Once you enter people's hearts, and become a part of their souls, it can not be as easily manipulated as a memory.

I have a message that I would like all to hear. My people, it is time we united and bow down to our origins. Without God we are lost. If I can travel to wherever the wind blows and touch the hearts of the young and old. If I can journey to wherever the wind blows, and heal the sick with a gentle kiss. If I can voyage to wherever the wind blows, and give truth to the misguided. Then let my words travel, journey, and voyage for me. It is time that we unmasked ourselves and challenge the pretentious façade of Society. The illusion is not real. I repeat, the illusion is not real.

Wherever the wind blows comes from the concept that there is not an inhabited place on this planet, that the wind does not blow. The wind blows bringing with it Life. Let my words travel wherever the wind blows. Let it bring Life. Let it become Life. Let it be a message to uplift the hearts of those who cherish the promise of Life. Thank you.

Carlos Bellamy

I. Reflections Of A Warrior

"My greatest fault was that I didn't value independent thought."
'Johnnie Ross'

Carlos Bellamy

Wherever The Wind Blows
40 years, day and night
to contemplate an egregious plight.

Sunshine is a seldom thing
prayed for but usually unseen.
Through it all we never complain.
Who knows pain, like those of us who remain
without an umbrella for the coming rain?
Console my soul with street rhymes of better times.
In a dark hole by a dark design.
Although alive, considered a walking chalkline.
The deaf and blind give hand signs
of signs from Jehovah Divine.
No one knows the perils of the roads the future holds.
As for me...I'm wherever the wind blows.
And to what end do we meet
if we travel the road beaten by many feet?
Is it a crime to be unique?
Or does the crime come when the unique
are made common and plain, by the insane pain
of following the stains
of a mad mob simply for material gain?
Follow my toes, to a place hidden by insidious foes.
To a place where remorse and suffering shows.
As for me... I'm wherever the wind blows.
Hollow hearts filled with grief.
Dreamers sleep, oblivious to the crying concrete
unpleased and plagued by marching feet.
The flag flies high.
The infamous red, white, and the blue.
America! She's the cousin of Jezebel.
Hypocritical and untrue.
The dreams I was taught to pursue
became a nightmare. Who can care for a local crew
deceived to sip brew, selling and smoking weed
in need of a dollar or two?
Unchosen by Liberty.
Chased and chained by the hate of misunderstanding.
I can see my grandchildren, unborn but demanding.

66

Desperate for an answer
to why this world so cruel
mistreats a majority of the minority.
From out of the cement comes a wilted rose.
As for me…I'm wherever the wind blows.

L.O.S.

Carlos Bellamy

<u>You Can Call Me November</u>
dedicated to the chains of my curse...
November, the month that gave way
to my birth

I was once a monument. My visions critically acclaimed.
Now I'm a collection of dust
desperately hoping to be remembered.
I have no name! You can call me November.
My Ancestors' name, slain by the murderous hands of Cain.
Unable to assist Able cuz I was never enabled.
I became labeled with the illusions of ignorant Black fable.
The world should be warned
that the pride of scorn
is a coat greedily worn, but easily torn.
I have no name! You can call me November.
Now I'm a collection of dust
by December I'll be nothing
more than a gathering of rust.
A soldier does what he must.
Even when corrupt in Jehovah we trust.
'By Any Means!', the ghettoes cuss.
I have no name! You can call me November.
Forgotten like the beauty of Autumn.
My heart breathes and bleeds
loud screams like the crunch of September leaves.
Yet it's a silent sound, for no one answers me.
I am the howling of the wind.
I am the still quiet night.
I am the change that arrives with the promise of pain.
A reminder that Winter storms are soon to come.
I have no name! You can call me November.

L.O.S.

<u>Raise Your Hands</u>

I put my tears and soul in this poem.
The essence of God in physical form.
A prophet once blessed as a ghetto unicorn.
Only problem only Satan saw my horn.
He battled me, won and left me torn.
So I wandered forty days out of uniform.
Fornicated with Jezebel out of scorn.
Half retarded, mentally sick.
I use to refuse to resist, now I insist
that I embrace my own grace
half saint, half exorcist.
Out of a concave cave
onto the decks of a convex ship filled with slaves.
Ungodly dreams and holy visions.
Poetic tongues constantly spittin
with a precision
so intense it causes immense reminiscing.
Where the wind blows, my immortal toes
continuously step.
A cement rose, in the middle of a dark road.
Shoulders slouched form the burdens of a heavy load.
I'll show you the truth and what it demands.
The complex plans of an intelligent man.
So if you feel me, don't speak!
Just raise your hands.

L.O.S.

It Aint Been The Same

A resume defined within the realms
and rhythms of reason.
Thoughts manifested in forms needing
the power and purifying of four seasons.
Every since Adam left Eden
it aint been the same.
Its like we all limp leaning on canes.
Wimps scheming inorder to maintain.
Double-teaming with fake claims of false fame.
Lost chalk, erased names.
Double-faced games, illusions of pain.
Bruised pride, the aftermath of unreleased laughs.
Whatever happened to the past paths
of gravel traveled before dreams smashed
by a fast crash.
Yesterday I stashed yesterday's wrath.
Today my heart race. Today is a hard race.
Tomorrow maybe I'll embrace
the nemesis of tomorrow's hate.
A resume defined within
the realms and rhythms of reason.
Thoughts manifested in forms needing
the power and purifying of four seasons.
Every since Adam left Eden
it aint been the same.

L.O.S.

It Never Ends

Jehovah it seems I'm alone
so I sing a song
about a soldier with no shoulder to lean on.
Immortalized, I survive in the mindz of friends.
So even if I die, it never ends.
The rewards and cheers of sin
nothing but false claps trapped within.
Every thought of me
that roams the corridors of your mentality
consistently brings me back
with a fierceness instantly
intertwined with the vividity of a validity
that dines with the after-life
that blinds you with a spiritual insight
to the roads of old, often told
before man strayed from the path.
Refusing to unleash the wrath.
I contain it! My tears a subtle reply
to 'Hell on Earth' seen with a carnal eye.
My reason 2 cry, its just too sad
cuz even my last laugh—a sarcastic sound
heard from 72 inches under ground.
In the end, my only sin
was my arrogant refusal to pass the truth around.
It was a much needed adjective to an unseen noun.
It never ends.

L.O.S.

I Hardly Hurt

I hardly hurt when I think of Yesterday's pain.
The flames from Wordly rain.
The change that never took place.
The things that never took form.
Often torn from an abundance of scorn.
I didn't choose to be burn.
I hardly hurt when my heart becomes stiff.
For me the misery doesn't exist.
My emotions contained, bottled-up.
In the end, the efforts of my pen
too pure and tough to be corrupt.
From out of the dust
with a gentle immaterial touch.
My greatest crime, my refusal to be hushed.
I hardly hurt, need I repeat how I feel?
I hardly hurt, need I repeat my tears are real?
I hardly hurt, now do you get the deal?
A storm's coming
I shall run, no wait—I'll stay and get wet.
After all I hardly hurt.
Jahweh, return me to the dirt.
I pray you first release the hurt
caused by this unclean planet Earth.

L.O.S.

I Have Seen This Before

As I sit here
my thoughts wander towards death.
I have seen this valley many times before.
But it has become apparent
that I will soon journey.
Preparations hastened and yet unmade.
Who knows why the wind blows?
I take a step forward, travelling behind me.
As the Earth rotates and moves
my dream alludes me.
To be free, a notion felt never to be seen.
To be pure, a holy gesture in this ungodly world.
My success lies within my failures.
My thoughts composes me.
A concrete rose eroded by bacteria and mold.
Truth be told, lies are sweet to hear.
My ears bleed from the things I've seen.
Tears released, only to be captured
and tormented by the Hearts of Men.
As I sit here
my thoughts wander towards death.
I have seen this valley many times before.
But it has become apparent
that I will soon journey.

L.O.S.

They Never Knew Me

Happy days I have seen.
But my past has been quarantined
as if such a serene scene
wasn't meant to be claimed
by a self-proclaimed King.
Even the best fail and fall.
Twice-told tales of jail and alcohol.
The gray cells of prison walls.
Strangers to my heart!
They never knew me.
Life in the fast lane after dark!
They never knew me.
approached with a proposal of atrocious deeds.
Stare close into my pupils
with a fierce intensity.
Why should I ride for you
and violate my creed?
Why should I lie for you
And destroy the 'Most High' seeds?
They never knew me.
To know me is to come to love me.
To love me is to understand me.
The story of my life…
misunderstood…
by even me at times. Whisper it with me!
THEY NEVER KNEW ME.
They Never Knew Me.
they never knew me.

L.O.S.

I Never Did

I never did ask for the company of hate.
Leave me in the solitude of yesterday.
I never did ask to be acquainted with stress.
Leave me undisturbed and let me rest.
A misery left alone
searches for someone to grab.
Insidious stabs, ungodly flesh wounds and dark paths.
Overcrowded tombs, the untouched wombs
of future wives.
My skin crawls, as I go where the wind blows.
I never did open any sealed windows.
Shattered glass, unasked for pain.
Bits and pieces, memories of broken frames.
I never did...
I never did...
...I never did.

L.O.S.

Carlos Bellamy

<u>Loyalty Less Than Love</u>
**In life certain principles may conflict with one another.
It is then that we must choose, which is the greater.**

I gave you my love, my life
and all that comes with such things.
I gave you my trust, my sight
and a key to unlock my dreams.
You gave me hope, along with a desire to live.
You gave me a promise
that life could never give.
You promised to be there.
You promised never to leave me.
Through thick and thin. Til death do us part.
What happened to that?
You promised to assist me.
You promised to grow old and reminisce with me.
Did you honestly forget all that?
I would have died for you!
Went to court and lied for you!
And for me, you would've done the same.
It seems strange that I no longer mention yo name
other than a passing thought
of getting crossed by this dirty street game.

L.O.S.

<u>Before Ashes Burn</u>

Before ashes burn, it seems the world turn
at a peaceful pace.
Joy brings happiness, because he is married to fate.
Yards full of grass, green and nicely trimmed.
Houses full of laughs, safely stored within.
A street car named hope, boasts of better times.
We joke with our friend, impervious to sinister signs.
After ashes burn, it seems the world turn
at a belligerent rate.
Joy no longer visits this accursed place.
That infamous villain hate, has seduced the widow fate.
Divorced. Broken homes breeds confusion and deceit.
Hate begot lunacy and anger, seeds of a thief.
The grass once green and trimmed has died.
Dreadfully brown, they feebly lay devoid of pride.
Before ashes burn it seems
we can achieve our greatest dreams.
After ashes burn it becomes clear
that to see is to suffer and shed a tear.
Before ashes burn, we have no reason 2 cry.
After ashes burn, it feels as if we live 2 die.

L.O.S.

Carlos Bellamy

<u>Never Meant To Cause You No Pain</u>
dedicated to my loving mother

I love you Ma, with all my heart and soul.
I know it seems like I've lost control
but my dreams were bold.
I chased them. Against all odds—Heaven knows.
Now the pain is two-fold.
The worse pain comes from hurting you.
I know you wanted the best for me.
And I feel as if I've disappointed you.
Your sacrifices did not go unnoticed.
Nowadays, I focus on the explosive
Dosage of love that you issued in doses.
Ma, how can I even ask to be forgave?
How can I convince you that I've changed my ways?
You gave me life. I gave you pain.
You gave me love. I gave you pain.
You are the reason I'm able to write.
And I thank you for it.
Never meant to make you cry.
Never had the chance to say goodbye.
Never meant to cause such a change.
Never meant to cause you no pain.

L.O.S.

A Brother To Me
dedicated to Bube 2
You're more than a brother

How do I say what I would like to say?
Don't know how to say what I must say.
But I have to compose this.
I have to put my heart and soul in this.
Bryan, you are more than a brother to me.
Where I am weak you are strong.
You are my crutch in times of need.
I know I have burdened you with my tears.
When it comes to this penitentiary pain
if it wasn't for you
I would have probably surrendered to the madness.
Bryan, you are more than a brother to me.
You are a friend. You are an advisor.
You are a reflection of the goodness
that lies within us all.
Bryan, you are more than a brother to me.
When thugz cry...you know the story.
Pac has moved my heart many times.
You inspired me when he could not.
And for that, I thank you.
Bryan, you are more than a brother to me.

L.O.S.

Carlos Bellamy

<u>Look At Me Brother</u>
written in response to Rabil's
Who Knows Pain?
Touch Ones.

Rabil, brother you once asked who knows pain.
You answered your question under duress, stress, and strain.
At the risk of loss, but instead you found the grain of gain.
Who knows pain? Look at me brother. I know pain.
A soldier stranded in sand dunes without a platoon.
Who knows pain? Look at me brother. I know pain.
If to suffer is to see, then to feel is to know pain.
I know pain for I have touched the flames.
I have walked the sullen roads, only to be drenched with rain.
Who knows pain? Look at me brother. I know pain.
Who knows pain? Look at me brother. I am pain.
Suffer my pain!
See my pain!
Feel my pain!
Know my pain!
Look at me brother, for I am pain.

L.O.S.

<u>What Are Friends For?</u>
**dedicated to the best friends
that I knew in this lifetime.**

Pissed-off at the World, I didn't ask for much.
A few hugz, a lil love—and a gentle touch.
Mad for the last 25 yearz. That's like all my life.
Can you wipe away these penitentiary tearz?
And give me some insight?
Can you help ease the pain on a lonely night?
Can you only help to settle an unsettled score?
After all, what are friends for?
Lost souls recently postponed.
Deprived of a shoulder, on which to lean on.
Ant I'm sorry you're gone.
I loved you like a brother.
My heart is now your home.
It is true, best friends are hard to find.
Mike I'm sorry I haven't called you in all this time.
What could I say except I failed.
And I'm destined to do time!
I didn't want to put you in a position
not to be there.
So out of my alleged care
I personally put you in a position
not to be there.
I made sure you wasn't there.
A promise kept. Judas! A name unspoke.
I'm trying to hold on
but the wind comes and snatches my hope.
I thought we would survive. whisper it! Me and you.
I thought I had learned from the first two.
All I learned was my best friend wasn't you.
It is true, best friends are hard to find.
I might not see another one in this lifetime.

L.O.S.

The Baddest Biggest 'B' I Know
In memory of
Ralph 'Big Bee' Bellamy

Dear Ralph, I miss you—literally.
Or should I say I literally missed you.
Our paths never crossed.
As I compose this work of art
a spirit moves me.
My pen once rude and disobedient
has suddenly become graceful
subjected to the whims of obeisance.
Live on and live long.
Live righteous
and you can live in me.
The baddest biggest 'B' I know.
What was the definition of your 'B'?
Was it the big boom of Bellamy?
Or were you the mate of a Queen Bee?
An elegant symbol of diligence.
Feeding on pollen and nectar.
The storer of honey.
Live on and live long.
Live righteous
and you can live in me.
The baddest biggest "B' I know.
Although I never knew you.
Your blood runz in my veins.
Black sheep without a family.
Your blood runz in my veins.
In my heart, I will carry you as family!
Your blood runz in my veins.
Live on and live long.
Live righteous
and you can live in me.
The baddest biggest 'B' I know.
Ralph, you're not dead.
You live in me.
My heart pumps your blood.
My tongue utter your words.

"I Aint Mad...
Freedom never reign.
I Am Somebody...
emptiness, is the pain."
Live on and live long.
Live righteous
and you can live in me.
The baddest biggest 'B' I know.
A message of truth
directed to the youth.
Sent through me
from 'Big Bee'.
'Read and free your minds
without the gift of knowledge
we are all blind.'
Rest In Peace.
To Ralph 'Big Bee'
The baddest biggest 'B' I know.

L.O.S.

II. Conscious Thoughts

"If we continuously embrace the concepts of 'an eye for an eye',
pretty soon we will all be blind."
L.O.S

<u>The Bearer Of Truth</u>
a message to self.

The bearer of truth
is despised in this world of lies.
Often hated upon
and never well liked.
It's a struggle just to be.

L.O.S.

Make Me A Promise
Inspired by the poetic works of Assata Shakur.
dedicated to a movement forever felt.

Oh, America! Make me a promise.
Promise me that tomorrow you will
undo your atrocious deeds of yesterday.
Promise me that you will redefine liberty
inorder to include my people.
I will admit my kindred are lost.
I will also admit that we are confused.
But yet, we stumble on—in search of something.
America! Make me a promise.
A promise filled with dignity?
A promise of truth given in earnesty?
Don't look away from the mirror!
Look into it and confront your past.
For it is your past that has made you
who you are today.
How can you promise us anything
with the clarity of certainty
when all you wish to do is forget our ancestors?
We will never let you forget.
Are we wrong to be proud of our Heritage?
Return us if you want, America.
But first let us uncondition our minds.
You have corrupted us America.
America! Make me a promise.
Promise me that you will leave Africa alone.
Promise me that you will remove your
abusive thieving hands from our Mother.
Let her grieve for what she has lost.
Let her rejoice over what she will soon gain.
America! Make me a promise.
Promise me that you'll keep your promise.
Without your word America, you are worthless.
Even if you promise me all that I ask of you
who's to say that you will keep your promises?
Hold on, now before you start grabbing
your water hoses, America

you have been known to deceive.
Hold on, now before you pass new laws
targeted at my people
America, you have been known to deceive.
The incarceration of lost souls.
Only in America.
America! Make me a promise.

L.O.S.

<u>Stolen Children</u>

Stolen children, are we all awake?
Survivors of hardship and heartaches.
Now's the time to rise and yell.
A yell that demands release from earthly hell.
Out of these hypocritical foreign doors.
Send us back to Africa, to our Mother's corridors.
Stolen children, are we all aware?
Survivors of starved sharks, we never had our share.
So how can we choose to remain in our kidnapper's care?
If you ask me, it was meant for us to return.
To return home. Not alone, but with legions of signs
and artifacts, of when Blacks reigned during times
when the Western world was blind.
Stolen children, come! Rally to my call!
The aftermath of our treacherous fall
shall be to rise up and stand tall.
Mother, can we talk to you?
Mother, will you welcome and accept us back?
Mother, will you ignore our differences
and embrace our similarities?
For although we were stolen
and sold by our own brothers
we are still rightfully and truly yours.

L.O.S.

The Illusions Of Peace
Inspired by the works of Assata Shakur.
dedicated to a movement forever felt.

My earliest memory is the illusions of peace.
My laughter unheard.
My childhood tears unseen.
Educated not to think, but to react.
Educated not to learn, but to pass by.
Educated to be uneducated.
Educated not to be educated at all.
Discontent with what once was.
At odds with what is.
Determined to fight for what will be.
My eyes, a vessel to understanding.
But the screams of death has left me deaf.
My hands...
Oh! My small calloused hands.
They were intended as tools to build and restore.
But now all they do is hold on to prison bars
as they attempt to hold together my broken heart.

L.O.S.

Carlos Bellamy

<u>**Somebody Answer Me!**</u>
Inspired by the works of Assata Shakur
dedicated to a movement forever felt.

Am I wrong for wanting more?
Am I bad for not believing that every opened door
should not necessarily be stepped through?
Am I out of pocket to feel hurt?
To feel as if my life has no worth?
Somebody answer me! Answer soon.
Am I wrong for desiring dreams?
Am I bad because uncertain things
has bought penitentiary scenes
to poison my well-being?
Am I out of pocket to feel misery?
To feel as if my future is ashamed
to see me approach?
Somebody answer me! Answer soon.
I can hear the ghostly painz of yesterday.
The echoes of a panthers roar.
Are we wrong to struggle on?
Are we bad because we search for a new path?
Are we out of pocket to feel
that your alleged liberty isn't real?
Somebody answer me! Answer soon.

L.O.S.

Yesterday I Sang a Song

Yesterday I sang a song
but the song was not mine.
The song was one of freedom.
The song was one of justice.
The song was one of liberty.
Things that are unseen
but still we constantly dream
that for us, one day they will exist.
I often reminisce of a night shift
where I sang a song of misery and bliss.
But the song I sang was not mine.
It belonged to my ancestoral line.
Picture my heritage all crying.
Those of my genetics singing while dying.
Yesterday I sang a song.
It was short and long.
It spoke of dark nights and bright dawns.
It was a song of beauty and peace.
It was a song of ugliness and war.
Yesterday I sang a song.
but the song was not mine.
The song was yours.
The song was ours.
We sang together.
Yesterday we sang a song.
The song was not only ours
it was also our ancestors song.
A song of hope.
A song of promise.
A song of future triumph.
Yesterday we sang a song.
And the world listened.
Crying with us we all sung a song.
A song that was not ours.
A song that belonged to the past
A song that belonged to the future.
A song sung in the present
with the strength of yesterday and tomorrow.

Carlos Bellamy

Yesterday I sang a song
but the song was not mine.

L.O.S.

Lost Tribes
In recognition to the native tribes.
Although lost, you are remembered.

We shall introduce ourselves
with the coming of the winds.
The arrival of the storm.
We are a lost tribe.
Nameless now, but not so
when we were first born.
Our kindness to the pilgrims
was insidiously repaid
by vicious lies
that disrupted our tribes
and brought about the exploitation
of African slaves.
We shall introduce ourselves
with the approach of the rain.
Columbus did not discover us.
An intruder on our soil
it was we who discovered him.
Along with multiple atrocities
and unexplicable pain.
Our land was pilfered and stolen.
Our names were lost.
We struggle to keep our culture intact.
And we do so no matter the cost.
Herded-up like cattle.
Reservations is where they placed us.
History has taught us a lesson.
Beware who we trust.
Who are we you ask?
I'll tell you who we are not.
We are not from India.
So why do you call us Indians?
We do not call our land America.
So why do you call us Native Americans?
We do not recognize the name of Amerigo Vespucci.
We shall introduce ourselves
with the advancing of the shining sun.

93

Carlos Bellamy

Remember the Shawnees.
Remember the Pawnees.
Remember the Utes.
Remember the Aztecs.
Remember the Sioux.
Remember the Blackfoot.
Remember the Apache.
Remember the Navaho.
Remember the Crow.
Remember the Incas.
Remember the Hurons.
Remember the Seneca.
Remember the Oneida.
Remember the Mohawk.
Remember the Cheyenne.
Remember the Dakota.
Remember the Arapaho.
Remember the Cherokee.
Remember the Iriquois.
Remember the Maya.
Remember the Chippewa.
Remember the Ojibwa.
Remember the Seminoles.
Remember the Cayuga.
Remember the Mahican.
Remember the Onondaga.
Remember the Tuscarora.
Remember the Illinois.
Remember the Mohegan.
We are the lost tribes.
Remember those who I have named
and those who I have not named.
Remember us all.
We are the Lost Tribes.
Witness our pain.
Feel our sorrow.
We struggle still.
Recognize and remember.
That is all that we ask of you.

L.O.S.

Only Lord Knows Why
**written in sincerity
so whenever you feeling unusually blue
embrace these words dedicated
especially for you.**

Listen! Can you hear the rain?
Here comes a storm
bringing with it frustration and pain.
Let not despair nor distress enter your shelter.
Hey you! Look into the mirror.
For in your eyes I see a
relentless river that runs continuously.
Hey You! Keep looking.
For in your smile I see sunrays
that warm consistently.
Let not your head drop, droop, or hang.
Lift it high, inorder to stare adversity in its eye.
Beautiful Black Woman, we must struggle on
or else our future will die.
Only Lord knows why.
Your tears are unshed.
With the stroke of this pen I cry for two.
Lets look past the surface and glance at your soul.
Take comfort and be consoled
for your hardships are as one with Job.
Need we travel a biblical road?
Remember Jonah and that beast of a whale?
Remember Noah and the near sacrifice of his child?
Remember the tumultuous tribulations of Esther?
Let not your head drop, droop, or hang.
Lift it high, inorder to stare adversity in its eye.
Beautiful Black Woman, we must struggle on
or else our future will die.
Only Lord Knows why.
When I see you I see traces of our Ancestors.
I see the determination of
Harriet Tubman and Sojourner Truth.
I see the endurance of
Althea Gibson.

95

I see the poetic hearts of
Gwendylon Brooks and Maya Angelou.
I see the outrage and stubbornness of
Rosa Parks.
I see shadows of
Phyliss Wheatley.
I see shadows of
Lorraine Hansberry.
I see shadows of
Nikki Giovanni.
Let not your head drop, droop, or hang.
Lift it high, inorder to stare adversity in its eye.
Beautiful Black Woman, we must struggle on
or else our future will die.
Only Lord knows why.

L.O.S.

<u>Queens</u>
A Woman's Anthem

Yesterday's Queens, your names reign supreme.
It's the simplest things
that moves me to support all you do.
Lets paint a picture, something ancient but new.
An elegant portrait, beautiful and true.
No matter the price, life lies within you.
Today's Queens, your dreams
have become a promise to me.
I was lost until I saw what you kept within.
A bright light of hope, never to be dimmed.
Continue lying down seeds
nurture whats to come
while preserving what is, and what shall soon be.
Tomorrow's Queens, it seems no one understands.
Although I am a man
I have listened and if it helps
I propose and plan
to give you not only my left
but also my right hand.
Struggle on, no matter the hurt.
Your sacrifices could never be a curse.
One day soon it will have its worth.
It is then that the Queens
of yesterday…of today…of tomorrow
shall blend and cause a trend
that will unite the harmony within.

L.O.S.

Living Our Struggle

My tongue is numb from divine prophecies.
The blind inconsistencies of multiple societies
is a cavity in my tooth.
I went to the dentist searching for the truth.
But it was like Beruit.
Chaos and disorder.
My soul continuously thirsts for water.
Can I sip from this puddle at my feet?
Or at least eat
something other than Society's foul meat?
Self-proclaimed scholars
misdirected and uneducated in college.
The tree of knowledge withered and dead.
Premonitions of bloodstainz where I lay my head.
Chained to these pools of red
by a thin thread.
Travel within to face the dread.
My life of sin
is like a wife who never makes amendz
constantly attackin again and again.
Will one of uz have 2 die, befoe it endz?
Now they question me how real?
As if though I was possessed and skilled
With insidious intentions concealed.
So I spit with a speed intense and furious
my creed so serious
it will make an atheist believe, or else go delirious.
Logarithms of logic
out of rhythm, an underground hobbit.
My spiritual audit coincides with the essence of church.
Picture me borderline beserk.
Standing on this planet Earth
with my head towards the dirt
hands up to shield the hurt.
I've been in pain
every since I've seen the chainz.
But when I attempt to change
the world views me as being deranged.

So I sit back, laid-back like
its aiight if I lose this fight
but tomorrow night, or the next night
when I continue my plight
if I lose the scuffle
my only rebuttal
is if you remember me
for living our struggle.

L.O.S.

Carlos Bellamy

A Deadman's Ghetto Creed

Poverty-stricken lives, that strives
off 43rd street highs.
In case you didn't notice
its hard for me. I can't focus.
Most of my guys dreams are hopeless.
Weight-shifters who scream
'the white man's bogus!'
Stop!!! Stop it!
Stop pointing the finger at another.
We need to uplift each other.
Pick up one another
embracing like brothers.
Or else we destined to leave our Mothers
with the tired of crying tears
with the nobody loves us fears
with the aint no reason for cheers.
Bottled beers. Empty dime bags.
Unpicked-up trash.
A newborn unheard life woes.
An old man's unseen death throes.
Lets sojourn on my ghetto block.
Where the disillusioned place glory in glocs.
With an economy based on white rocks.
Where aint no love for local cops.
Car speakers bumping something hot.
Probably the greatest of 2-Pac.
Young knaves unafraid of the grave.
Might be thinking there's a better place
and not only for those who behave.
Ask Mike, 'They don't really care.'
We protest with overgrown hair.
Foodstamps. Cut-off welfare.
Underfed children
oblivious to the source
of their next meal.
The epitomy of Society's ills.
They say crack kills.
So does neglect.

I refuse to accept an early death.
Not without a few words
being recorded and heard.
I'm the pain of all who breathes and bleed.
Pass me on to your seeds.
My words give oxygen to 'em like trees.
And if I fall
don't step on these November leaves.
Pick me up!
And for you, I'll do the same indeed.
This here—is a deadman's ghetto creed.

L.O.S.

Carlos Bellamy

Convicted In The Womb
inspired by the book 'Convicted in the Womb'
by Carl Upchurch. We thank you Carl
for empowering us.

I am here today to tell you
that I was convicted in the womb.
Before I even inhaled my first breath
I was sentenced to poverty and racism.
Before I even inhaled my first breath
I was sentenced to poverty and racism.
Before I even released my first scream
I was sentenced to social inequities.
Before I even shed my first tear
I was sentenced to anger and hopelessness.
Unknowingly I chose to embrace
the hatred that was provided.
Later on, realizing that there was a better way
but unable to successfully
hurdle the obstacles
that was surreptitiously placed on my path.
I am here today to tell you
that I was doomed
to be convicted in the womb.
Sealed inside an airless tomb.
Misery and mayhem looked upon my soul
with smiling faces.
Comforted by the sight of me.
Laughing, thrilled to see
that someone, somewhere
was worse off than them.
They are long gone.
But I still hear the mockery
of their laughter.
Laugh no more!
Silence your insidious hearts!
A Council for Urban Peace and Justice.
Hope renewed. We thank you Carl.
Ripples of the summit
a dim memory.

Hope stolen.
Snatched away by the thieving hands
of confusion and deceit.
America, what have you done to us?
Only what we have allowed you to do.
Where are our leaders?
No I am not referring to them.
Where are our leaders?
No one wants to hear my voice.
So I'll scream louder!
Then whisper silently.
Where are our leaders?
We are our leaders
and we must stand up
and lead ourselves.

L.O.S.

Burn Me Along With My Beliefs
inspired by James Baldwin
'The Fire Next Time'

Burn me along with my beliefs.
For unlike you I am willing to perish
not by water, but fire
if I am ever proven wrong.
My beliefs are not based upon
the perception of lies.
I am my own foundation.
Secure in the knowledge of self.
If I am to blame for my conditioning
who's to blame for my unconditioning?
The rhetorics of 'the infamous pointing finger.'
The shrinking of an individual.
Illusions of old currently embraced.
Universal truths continuously unfaced.
A human race with no finish line in sight.
Unamerican as America itself.
Refuge taken in a delusion.
Go ahead, pick your shelter.
Will it be religion or crime?
Politics or a picket sign?
Hypocritical morality or wanton disregard
for the principles of life?
America, these are your beliefs.
And they are yours to believe in.
However foolish they may seem to me.
All I ask is that if you disagree with me.
Burn me along with my beliefs.

L.O.S.

The Greatest Journey

The greatest journey a man can take
is to travel the road of truth.
Out of the wilderness of sleep
instantly awaken to the ethos of love.
It takes strength to realize
you've been deprived.
The coldest season is the warmest one yet.
To die with regret is to die incomplete.
To live befriended by misery and lunacy
the constant companions of stress
is to live alone, lonely and incomplete.
I cherish what the world rejects
—the simple things.
Guilty—my only sin
I never grieved the laws of Society.
Away with me!
Make room for those to come.
I SEE MILLIONS!
The weakest amongst them unafraid.
I SEE ONE!
A prophet destined to die untimely.
The righteous step towards an unrighteous death
aware that even the righteous must hold
their breath, in this ungodly place.
Nevertheless, the greatest journey
a man can make
is to travel the road of truth.

L.O.S.

Invisible Man
inspired by Ralph Ellison's powerful novel.

I traveled to the borders of chaos.
Stunned, shocked, and appalled by what I saw
I expeditiously jumped back to Society's sanity.
And yet, I was somehow compelled to return.
Unwritten testaments of a time unheard.
History lessons unread and never once heard.
Manipulated to embrace the hatred of hard times.
Ill-fated and aggravated I'm tempted to resign
from the constant crying, the daily trying,
the tiredness of the smell of the dying,
the futile attempts of flying,
the failure to quiet the tortured
souls that are frying.
How can I see but remain unseen?
How can I hear agonizing yells
without anyone releasing a scream?
How can I dream as if I was asleep?
In a trance so deep
that to awaken is to embrace defeat.
I am invisible that's how!
The mirror tells no lies. I am an invisible man.
Society refuses to see me.
I am an invisible man.
Am I a crime that refuses to be acknowledged?
If so, enhance the opticals!
I will be acknowledged.
Enlighten the sixth sense, the third eye!
I will be acknowledged.
Nevertheless, Society cannot see me...
...I am an invisible man.

L.O.S.

When Silence Speaks
silence speaks a thousand words.

When silence speaks
it composes the lyrics
to the songs of
larks, sparrows, robins
and nightingales.
When silence speaks
the wise man listens
while the fool continues to talk.
When silence speaks
the principles of love instantly defined.
The metaphors of life born.
Strategic similes adopted.
Parented by patience and virtue.
Three moves from checkmate
on an untouched chessboard.
When silence speaks
lessons are learned.
Silence speaks a thousand words.
Each one unique, elegant
informative and enlightening.
When silence speaks
hearts are moved
caressed by heavenly hands.
When silence speaks
beauty is described.

L.O.S.

A Distant Thought

A distant thought, an action meant to last.
Revelations of times unseen
infractions from the past.
An atrocity seen in a moment of weakness.
What ought to be, is not what is.
What's lost to me, is not for hatred to give.
My reasons to live
reciprocals of my thirsts to die.
Dead but reborn.
Alive with a new vigor.
A new strength.
A truth universally known
is found once error has been shown.
My last poem, shall be my last song.
Resuscitated full blown from a time zone
where the evil of people was noticed
as a problem of future clones.
A quoted thought by Johnnie Ross
"I will not let you turn my truth
into an untruth, to satisfy your
quest for truth."

Quoted thought by Johnnie Ross

L.O.S.

<u>Drop Science</u>
**In hopes that one day
the masses shall awaken.**

Ignorance is nothing new.
Fools are many, while the wise are few.
Remain true to untrue principles.
I denounce the streetz.
Just as surely, the streets denounce me.
Although I've seen the chaos of the streetz
I'm not from the streetz.
My origins is amongst the Heavens.
Shining stars dimmed by an abyss of hate.
The hearts of men, condemned to trace
the contours of past mistakes.
Lying on the concrete, as my soul bleeds
from the fictious creed
of envy, lust, and greed.
A century of unwise lies. Illogical alibis.
The lives of the self-proclaimed wise.
Blind eyes stitched together.
Unopened doors. Paralyzed feet.
Hell on Earth nothing unique.
Send me underneath, above
where my fellow prophets sleep.
I pity those who boast of things
that have no worth.
Altered realities, hypocritical aborted births.
Insignificant emphasis on color.
I am black! I am white! I am red!
I am yellow! I am brown! I am all!!!
Hebrews, Christians, and Jews
in truth we form an alliance.
Living our struggle, I drop science.

L.O.S.

Carlos Bellamy

Corridors Of A Cell
**dedicated to all those trapped
in the realms of hate. Maybe this
will inspire yal to break the cycle.**

I often brood as I consume food
with a Hebrew's mood.
Unaffected, but viciously disrespected
whenever I mention dreams of a freedom neglected.
If this is a false reality
can truth be found?
With my right ear I can hear
a horrible heart-broken sound.
The Dr. says Mother Africa is calling.
I repeat, Dear Margaret says
Mother Africa is calling.
But who will listen
and make it their lifetime mission
to change and rearrange the positions
of the young minds?
Blind, continuously doing time.
Birth certificates unsigned.
Death warrants issued for alleged crimes.
Broken glass. Shattered hearts.
Bits and pieces of corridors frightfully dark.
In my lifespan I followed man
so I failed.
The unclean screams of Hell.
Twice-told tales
of brave hearts who rebelled.
The flames engulf my physical shell.
Witness my pain
within the corridors of a cell.

L.O.S.

Broke Jokes
The wasted youth, hate the truth.
Rest to all my soldiers who fell.
I remain on the field, where the battle is held.

Broke jokes of hope and fast cash.
Thin broke jokes of thin hope in a thin stash.
Although it's a struggle, still I rise.
Still I surpass.
The choices we make we understand in the past tense.
Obsessed and possessed with nomadic notions
of the fusia fence of the future tense.
Society's incess uncloaked by the modern incense
of radio's and T.V. shows.
Instead of cafes and bookstoes
black neighborhoods plagued with
pool halls and liqua stoes
currency exchanges and pawn shops.
We need to change the stainz of our overworn socks.
If not, let us uncock glocs
or at least re-aim the thangz
away from our own black brainz
and towards Society's untouched chainz.
Broke jokes of hope
do we deserve to be laughed at?
Faith floatz from under our ghetto curbs
up into heavenly skies amongst the birds.
True power is in the beauty of wordz.
As I continuously travel this old weary road
I see memories of me.
Memories of uz and the paths we chose.
Stolen smiles lost
The epiteph of a concrete rose.
Broke jokes of hope
we're left shivering in the cold.

L.O.S.

Carlos Bellamy

The Fifth Element
Dedicated to all who have succumbed
to the quest for peace.
It seems it's a concept we'll never reach.
Nevertheless, we continue to seek.

It is better to have loved and lossed
than to never have loved at all.
It is better to have had
the quality and companions of one
than to have had
the quantity and emptiness of all.
Or is it?
What is the use of protecting life
when you see whats done with it?
We save lives with the lies of killing lives
for the sole sake of our children and wives.
The future hides its face
not wanting a taste of our ignominous past.
Air blows with the haste of hate
as if to conceal the righteous path.
Fire burns into ash
that which can never last.
Water runs
drowning itself in a pernicious flood.
Earth, well earth it does what it does.
The fifth element touches me deep
for it is the unconditional power of love.

L.O.S.

<u>Unafraid Of The Dark</u>
Dedicated to Rosemary L. Bray

To take notice of the things we've never loved
is to truly appreciate what life is composed of.
My life an anathema to the ethos of Society.
My cynicism reason enough to quietly quiet me.
Pre-conditioned to prescribe to precarious conduct.
My demise a corollary of dirt
clothed by a contour of dust.
It hurts not to be able to trust.
It hurts to be coerced to embrace
what my heart considers corrupt.
The perusal of pretentious pundits.
The dissonance of diaphanous discourse.
Continues as an iconoclastic
to induce misanthropic behavior.
Pitch-black devoid of detail
lightless regions where suspicion and hatred dwell.
What does it take to awake from slumber?
My hunger to enlighten, a deed yet to be done.
My Ghostly Painz, a song yet to be sung.
My dreams, that of a negroe already hung.
Still I rise, still I dream on.
Unafraid of the dark
because the morning is soon to come.

L.O.S.

<u>Its Just Too Sad</u>

Its just too sad that money
makes men do such bad things.
Its just too sad that money
disillusion people as to what it really brings.
If you make money the basis of your living
it is then that you confine
yourself in a material prison.
Sure money is needed inorder to survive.
Society has made it that way.
If Society being evil chooses to mislead
why would a sane person continue to breathe
the filth that greed consistently breeds?
Its just too sad to think and reflect.
Idols of green, a spiritual death.
Another soldier's soul lost.
Its just too sad when I contemplate the cost.
I write to be heard and remembered for my work.
Money could never motivate me
to burn what I've learned from the church.
I write to release passions
upon this misguided Earth.
I write to bring a smile to a sad face.
I write to uncloud a dark heart.
Its just too sad
but to please the entire world
its just too hard.

L.O.S.

Dearest Doctor
Life is a paradox.
And I dedicate this to the contradictions within.

Dearest Doctor, can you tell me what is wrong?
I have feelings inside me
that I refuse to condone.
Constantly haunted by late night zones
from a time unwanted and unknown.
Images of a happy home
is what you say I need.
You say perhaps
I should follow a Christian's creed
and find something in which to believe.
Dearest Doctor, I don't mean to be rude.
But you talk as if I was one and not two.
You can't honestly blame me for my attitude.
Misery loves company. I choose solitude.
I have a personality split
and together we continuously co-exist.
He causes chaos and it appears
as if though I'm a misfit.
Speak louder Doctor, what you said I didn't hear.
You'll have to drown out the voices
which I've come to hold dear.
Oh! You say what I need is a Catholic ear near
to listen to my own insecurities
which I helplessly fear.
Dearest Doctor, enough talk is there a cure?
Something that has been declared sure
to wipe out these vicious thoughts, so unpure?
Doctor! Dearest Doctor, did you even hear me?

L.O.S.

Carlos Bellamy

<u>Hip-Hop Forever</u>
A tribute to Hip-Hop.
The side they don't wanna see.

Crowds full of people.
Young and old.
All races.
No borderlines. No limitations.
The latest kicks. Gold chains.
Fly clothes. Expensive cars.
Drug lords with guns.
Nah! It aint about that.
Self-love. Self-worth.
Unity.
We shall overcome.
Yeah, eventually.
A side unseen.
At least not televised
or promoted by political Kings.
Lyrical talents.
A gift provided, divinely inspired.
Escape the madness
but at the same time embrace the madness.
A language provided
to show the world what we've been through
what we go through
and the obstacles we'll have to
immediately hurdle tomorrow.
Yeah, Hip-Hop forever.

L.O.S.

Hey, That Aint Me!
inspired by Indie Arie

Don't need no jewelry
or the latest kicks to
define who I am.
Hey, that aint me!
Don't need no super-duper
fancy car
or no expensive clothes
to define who I am.
Hey, that aint me!
Don't need no token female
with his or hers furs
in a big house with
a lion that purs
to define who I am.
Hey, that aint me!
Don't need no job
with a six zero income
to define who I am.
Hey, that aint me!
All I need to define
who I am
is to travel within
and become who I am.

L.O.S.

<u>Passing By</u>
November, 26 1986
In memory of Harold Washington
dedicated to the birth of Catherine Antoinette Dansberry

Oh America! America!
Why have you forsaken
what you claim to believe in?
I, Harold, could've brought about
the change the Kennedy's wanted
the dream Martin spoke about
the vision Malcom once saw.
Now I'm nothing but a memory
just as they are.
As I pass by, I see a beautiful face.
Little one what is your name?
'They shall call me Catherine.'
Well then Catherine, know one thing.
Life is a paradox in which we must struggle.
My sweet dearest child
My precious birth of hope
My endearing sentiment of passion
Live and see and know this.
When death comes so shall enlightment.
'I see Harold, I'll keep that in mind.'

L.O.S.

<u>Play</u>

I dedicate this to the
father I never knew.
He left my mother
before I turned two.
Since I'm only eight
for him I have no hate.
I keep him in a secret place
where happy thoughts wait.
Just in case he returns.
My brother Al told me a story
where a million blacks
marched and screamed.
To free the youth was the theme.
But my brother says
it didn't mean a thing.
Cuz how can we be free
until we first learn that freedom
is more of a mindstate
than a physical thing.
I'm kinda confused
cuz I thought to be free
was to be able to play
wherever I wanted.
I guess that means I aint free.
Moms tell me to stay
close to the porch
cuz it aint safe nowhere else.
Since the gangs came
with the guns and drugs
I can't play where I love.
Around here it aint safe
to be in the parks after dark.
Not unless you aint
afraid of gunsparks.
Befoe I sleep
I pray so hard I often weep.
Lord can you please
bring my Daddy back to me?

Carlos Bellamy

> But first befoe you do that
> can you take the gangs away!
> Can you take the guns away!
> Can you take the drugs away!
> Can you take the crime away!
> All I want is a place to play.
> Cuz if you don't
> where can a kid play?

L.O.S.

<u>Time</u>

What can be greater than time?
Immortal warriors slain behind enemy lines.
Magnificent kingdoms, forgotten since they have lost their shine.
The young become wrinkled and bent.
Teary-eyed their children wonder where they went.
What can be greater than time?
Witness the metamorphasis, the strong suddenly weak.
Boisterous individuals hardpressed to whisper or speak.
Take a second to look under your feet.
You see them cracks? When it comes to time,
even concrete surrenders to defeat.
What can be greater than time?
In my life, I have met belligerent individuals.
I'm not tough! You're not tough!
Time is tough!
I haven't met anyone yet that can fade time.
What can be greater than time?
What can be greater than time,
but time itself?

L.O.S.

It Aint New To Me

A monument to the times it was written within.
The graces of my pen
brings to life the promises within.

Brother Malcom, as I sit here today I think of you.
There's only a few true who remember you as I do.
Your words touched ones.
Moving the hearts of the young
daughters and sons, of your grandchildren.
It aint new to me.
Brother Malcom, what happened to us as a whole?
At times it seems, Satan stole our lost souls.
Its hard to console the black hole
that has taken its toll.
It aint new to me.
Brother Malcom, we need you still.
We are without a leader that feels
the ills of society and the deity they concealed.
Our grief has taken the form of a small hill.
It aint new to me.
Brother Malcom, the seeds you planted
have wiltered and died.
Unfortunately, they never received water
or rain from the skies.
So I cry. Desperate to sing a melody.
Something optimistic, that will eliminate the misery.
Brother Malcom…
the hope you bought, it aint new to me.
The lessons you taught, it aint new to me.
The fruits we lossed, it aint new to me.
Brother Malcom, you're not new to me.

L.O.S.

III. The Harmony Of Hearts

"We will never fully understand the powers of love, and to what great measures we place trust in these concepts."

<u>Goodbye</u>
dedicated to half my heart, Nicole
inspired by Alicia Keys

How do I say goodbye
to a love that is eternal?
How do I say goodbye
to a love that is immortal?
Nicole, I still miss you.
You are the epitomy of a woman's worth.
I still love you with all my heart.
You are a part of my soul!
Is it still love, or is it attachment?
Five years of silent tears.
And still I love you.
How do I say goodbye?
If it makes you feel better
paint an imperfect picture
with me as the villain.
It was my fault that we both
felt the pain of heart-break.
Nicole, how do I say goodbye
when I still love you dearly?
I guess I need closure.
Forgive me for hurting you.
It took a lot of strength
for me to say that.
I've matured.
Nicole, how do I say goodbye
to a love that no longer exists for you
but that grows daily within me?
Am I disillusioned?
We both failed to take
the necessary measures
to restore what we once had.
How do I say goodbye?
For the love of you.
That is how I say goodbye.
Never meant to cause you no pain.
That is how I say goodbye.

Remember Me.
That is how I say goodbye.
The Heartbeat Of A Heart.
That is how I say goodbye.
In Honor Of A Lost Love.
That is how I say goodbye.
Never Will.
That is how I say goodbye.
Maybe our souls will be intertwined
in our next lifetimes.
Nicole…goodbye.

L.O.S.

Carlos Bellamy

Unspoken Heart
dedicated to a love I can never have.
my heart is yours

The possibility of love moves mountains within me.
The fact that our love could never exist
crushes mountains within me.
Let it be clear, when I speak of love
I speak of the hope of eternity.
Ocean waves caressing particles of sand.
The silhouette of the moon, glowing in dim places.
Even if you could never love me
My silent heart confesses a love for you.
My love buried in a grave of never could be's.
I fear reincarnation. It seems a curse to come back.
But I'd gladly return, if in the next lifetime
I'd be guaranteed the remotest chance
whether successful or not, to know your love.
I often forget our timing wasn't right.
I often forget we shouldn't see each other.
I often forget you're married with kids.
I often forget the notion that love hurts.
I often forget myself and become a single thought.
A single thought of you.
I often forget my heart even spoke.
Unspoken heart.

L.O.S.

I See Pieces Of Me In You
An unspoken heart still unspoken.

Not with your mouth, but with your eyes
you ask why am I attracted to you.
Its because you are similar
to a multitude of dreams
that only I have dreamed.
With each dream a different
part of you shines.
I see pieces of me in you.
The more I look upon you
the more beautiful you become.
I have been stunned and silenced
by your beauty.
Curiosity has forced me to be brave.
Would I know more about you?
I see pieces of me in you.
Your intellect stimulates my thoughts.
Would I know a reflection of your love?
Heaven knows
my eyes have been constantly rubbed.
But you are reality.
Thank God you are not a mirage.
You have unknowlingly won a place in my heart.
I see pieces of me in you.
I understand love
and I am aware that
I am not in love with you.
But I am in love
with the idea of loving you.

L.O.S.

Carlos Bellamy

My Heart Knows Love
**written after viewing
'Shakespeare in Love'**

I come forth today to testify
that my heart knows love.
Attachment has been abandoned.
Deserted on an unknown island.
My heart knows love.
Infatuation, buried in an unmarked grave.
Slain by the sword of Purity.
My heart knows love.
Lust has fled for his own safety.
A cowardly criminal that alludes Justice.
My heart knows love.
I bear witness in front of
Honesty and Truth.
That if ever the day comes
that finds the virtue of my heart
to be judged as false.
Then imprison me into the clutches of Fate.
The second cousin of Death.
Puncture my eyes!
And I'll still scream
my heart knows love.
Seize my ears!
And I'll still whisper
my heart knows love.
I risk life and limb.
Inhaling my last breath
inorder to confide in the
sanctuary of your bosom.
I write this in hopes of knowing your love.
In hopes of you becoming my love.
I would have my gentle heart
familiarize itself, with the acquaintance
of your every thought.
My love, my heart knows love
for my heart knows you.

L.O.S.

<u>Where Is My Special Place?</u>
inspired by the thought of love

Where is my special place?
Where am I allowed to seek shelter
when confronted by the whips of hate?
Where is my special place?
Where to can I run
when engulfed by misery?
Where is that place
that will erase the vindication of fate?
Turning back the hands of time
allowing a lost soul
to re-surface and make attempts
to re-gain a life once lost.
Where is my special place?
Where can I travel
inorder to find
celestial arms that wraps
around my humble heart
with a gentle touch?
Passion, leave me not to dreams!
Desire, lead me not to illusions!
Answer me true when I ask
where is my special place?

L.O.S.

Carlos Bellamy

<u>My Last Kiss</u>
inspired by Maria Oleza's 'The Last Kiss'

My last kiss
was not a good one.
But if I would have
known that my last kiss
would have been
my last kiss.
I would have made it
more sensuous
more pleasant
more romantic.
Encapturing two souls
intertwined in a dance
the melody of bliss.
I would have made it
…more.

L.O.S.

<u>Necessity of Perfection</u>
dedicated to Tina, a.k.a Shorty 'T'

Thoughts of a friend lost.
Heavens! Have you seen her?
Where could she be?
Dear sweet Tina, where did you come from?
I must confess, I missed you dearly.
Nowadays my love lies dormant and untouched.
Oracles of a silent love never told.
I love all
but few truly hear my heart's call.
Your timing couldn't have been better.
The promise of life instilled within this very letter.
To hear your voice once more
was to invade the skies and soar
was to be a lion releasing a mighty roar
was to be a ruby on the ocean floor
shining in the sun after being washed ashore.
My being parted from you once more
as Poe once said "nevermore, nevermore
…nevermore."

L.O.S.

Carlos Bellamy

<u>Sincerely</u>
Dedicated to Tashaun
Love, plenty much.

Your heart needed to be rebuilt.
I should've been there to
Chisel together the foundations.
That way, I could have made right
The wrongs caused by others.
That way, I could have made right
The wrongs caused by me.
You say you're scared to be alone.
But how can you possibly be alone?
Am I not present in the functioning
Of your mind, body, and soul?
If I am the light that eliminates the dark
If I am the rainbow that follows the rain
If I am the cure to heart-broke pain
If I am any of these, its only because
You have allowed me to be.
Without you in my life I am incomplete.
Sincerely.

L.O.S.

IV. Transferred Feelings

"If you begin by sacrificing yourself to those you love, you will end by hating those to whom you have sacrificed yourself."
'George Bernard Shaw'

Questions
written for Lil C

Questions. Unanswered questions.
Rhetorical questions.
The answers are already known. Check this out,
I got something on my dome. A few questions of my own.
Without my word what could I possibly be?
Without you trusting in me, what are you to me?
Without faith in us, where are we?
Answer those for me Boo, but before you do—
there's something I'd like to express to you.
The hurt deep, the pain intense extremely ugly.
To separate a father from his daughter,
the thought far from lovely.
I can hear rebellious screams from underneath and above me.
If I'm wrong, then I apologize. Tell me can you still love me?
If so, let gentle Da-zhonna come and hug me.
Ultimatums leads to peculiar positions. You've backed me against a wall.
I'm tempted to back you against a wall. If we go this route, our love
will be a monument waiting to break and fall. I'm tired of the lies,
the games, the negatives. Trina I need you. I propose everything unjust
let it be exposed. That way our love will be a concrete rose. I have no
reason to lie. To lie is to not live. Answer me this, do you think our
love is a lie? I'm telling you that our love can never be a lie. Answer
me this, are you willing to let our love die? I'm telling you, our love
is immortal it can never die.

L.O.S.

Before Us
for Bop

Although its complicated, Brittany I love you.
Although I've been gone since you were eight,
still I love you.
You're thirteen now.
About to be fourteen, almost grown now.
Let me tell you the ways I remember you and how.
Soft and sweet, like the twinkle in an eye.
Outgoing, smart, and kind of shy.
Remember the way I taught you how to share?
Remember stopping in the candy store after daycare?
I taught you the basic things.
The joy and happiness that love brings.
If I had to tell you what you mean to me
I couldn't possibly say it all.
For now, lets just say that my love explains it all.
Although life aint fair, it can never defeat us.
Nothing comes before us.
Although there's distance between us.
There's no one before us.

L.O.S.

Carlos Bellamy

A Spring Of Hope
written for Dello

Behold, the month of July brings forth a rose.
A spring of hope, promising life
where grass no longer grows.
DaShayne its plain for me to see
that without you there would be no me.
Caged birds sing sad songs of holding on.
When the smoke disappeared
you was near while everyone else was gone.
Stolen smiles and lost memories found and returned.
My love for you a fire that continuously burn.
As the world turns
let us reflect and reminisce.
The days of old when you done my chores
they were times of bliss.
I insist, indeed there would be no me without you.
Love and inspiration from above
received and delivered through you.
If I had to pick a season to describe you
I would choose winter.
My reason being, you're a blanket of snow
that comforts me and lets me know
to keep my head up, no matter which direction I go.
You mean a lot to me. Let us take time to pray.
Our Father, who guides us every day
who watches with a heavy heart as we go astray
together we pray
if its your will, let my sister and me
walk where the Angels lay.
Dear DaShayne, Happy Birthday.

L.O.S.

Thinking of You
Greeting card
written for Rochelle from Tojo

No matter how hard it gets
Thinking of you.
Thinking of us.
Your delicate touch
intimate, simple but yet deep.
Destinies collide as heavenly stars meet.
Unforgotten memories made
and kept in constant reach.
Remember me as I remember you
on my brother's couch sleep.
From hallway kisses
to thoughts of you as my Mrs.
Church bells wanted
perhaps soon to be seen.
Dedicated dreams
of white dresses and precious rings.
As we face the tribulations of fate
let us remember Today's promises that await
while forgetting Yesterday's race
of failure and hate.
Tears of joy bestowed upon us by Allah.
Sometimes I dream and my loved ones come to me.
When I see Kenashia
Thinking of you.
When I see Hezeakia
Thinking of you.
When I see Laqunanda
Thinking of you.
No matter how hard it gets.
Thinking of us...
Thinking of you.

L.O.S.

<u>Togetherness</u>
written for Tojo
dedicated to Rochelle

Togetherness.
The sun and sky.
The rise and set of light.
An epiphany of hope
within our sights.
The infinite heights of love
transcended in the form of a dove.
Togetherness.
The turtle and its shell.
Protected from the fear of the unknown.
The wind has blown
but shelter exists
within the bliss
of one another's grip.
Togetherness.
A fish in the sea.
In its element.
Oceans of honesty
loyal to the nature of time.
Togetherness.
An idea of everlasting complexity
found in a simple singular moment.
Togetherness.
You.
Me.
The concepts of us.
Intertwined in the arms of trust.
Togetherness.

L.O.S.

L.O.V.E
written 4 Tojo—dedicated to Rochelle

Love is the elements of kinship.
Personal ties intertwined.
Affection based upon assurance.
Oaths are solemn intents.
sincere forms of expression.
sacred words attested and inviolable.
Valor is the vindication of commitment.
The strength of virtue.
The courage of cooperation.
Eternity is the length of togetherness.
The etesian of summer winds.
The epoch of infinite ethos.
The duration of thinking of you.

L.O.S.

Carlos Bellamy

I Often Wish
written 4 Black

I often wish our time
together wasn't so short.
I often wish my words were not lost.
Maybe then I could easily
express how I feel.
I often wish I could see you every day.
Maybe then my sentiments would be
elaborately explained.
I often wish I could view my heart.
I would be viewing you.
You are my heart.
Without you it would be impossible
to define me.
Shiquila, I miss you so much.
Just wanna hear you laugh.
See your smile.
Be there to comfort you.
Just wanna keep in touch.
I love you.

L.O.S.

V. Songs Of Sanctuary

"All children paint like geniuses. What do we do to them that so
quickly
dulls this ability?"
'Picasso'

Haiku's

An Untimely Death
In the event of
an untimely death on my
body, do not cry.

My Tears
My reason 2 cry
was heard by deaf ears, so now
my tears reflect pain.

Beautiful Thoughts
Wherever the wind
blows, beautiful thoughts so goes.
My life has been touched.

L.O.S.

A Patriot's Poem

The symbolism of that evil eagle
is lost upon my ghetto people.
We were never seen as equal
by our counterparts with whips.
Mobbed-up on ships, starved and sick.
Sharks quick to follow the ships
well-fed for their wit.
The memorable dream that Martin seen
now a silent thing.
Hopes of sunshine, while drenched with rain.
Fears that yesterdays will remain
overshadowing today's pain.
If so, our tomorrow's are in vain.
My black vein
allegedly a stigma upon my brain.
But I defiantly claim
Society is the one uncleansed and stained.
Dear World!
Why can't you see with my eyes?
Dear Lord!
Why can't I see with my eyes?
I despise the lies that rise
derived from the hate that awaits
perpendicular figures parallel to Hell's gates.

L.O.S.

<u>Untitled</u>

Lately I bleed, as I try to conceive
of past deeds
and render them undone.
Immoral thieves, who perceived
of future greed
before the war was ever won.

Lately I cry, as I attempt to fly
above the sky
and beyond my dreams.
Questions of why, easily dodged with a lie
dismissed without a try
unanswered and never to be seen.

Lately my pen, dries up never to write again.
A Literary sin
to let talent waste.
A dark heart dimmed, without a grin
never to smile again
can be seen within my face.

L.O.S.

The Yard

As I walk the prison yard, at times it seems strange.
Life's no longer a game. I can feel the power of the pain.
The stains of pistols unchanged.
Nowadays its more than just a mental game.
I listen to my man, thinking he's the man
with a story similar to the next man.
As I walk the yard at times it seems strange to me.
Although trife I embrace this thug-life angrily.
The only danger to me, is the seeds of anger in me.
As I walk the yard dead in defiance
my loyalty is only to thoughts of an alliance.
My lifestory similar to a science.
L.O.S-ology, the study of hard aches and scrapes.
It seems to suffer is human fate.
Dead but still breathing, a silhouette with no shape.
I proposed to regret and ended up engaged to hate.
As I walk the yard I smile at the vision
that arrives with immense precision.
This yard cannot contain me.

L.O.S.

A Rally

A rally was to be held,
The cause serious and severe
so it must be upheld.
'We will not fail!' The leaders cried.
Hearing screams of somber sorrow
the peasants multiplied.
'A revolution! We will have a revolution!'
The leaders yelled and the crowd Responded.
Faced with a deliberate decision
the leaders left for night had come.
The crowd boiling over with sentiments
of anger and frustration made a belligerent move.
Unorganized, the common men
took to the field baring arms.
They left the field stiff corpses
held in their wives arms.
The next morn as the widows mourned
a rally was to be held.
The leaders was asked to be held accountable
for the dead and those in jail.
The leaders simply responded
'We were sleep.'

L.O.S.

A Ghetto Prayer

Lord, I come humble
and in need of your help.
I acknowledge you as the 'Most High'
the Supreme Being.
Lead me down the path that is just.
Lead me down the road that is
ornamented by your holy word.
Lead me not astray.
Let not temptation have any power
when it comes my way.
Lord God, I ask for guidance.
Guide me away from the darkness of drugs.
Guide me away from the glamour of guns.
Guide me away from the gimmick of gangs.
Guide me away from the chivalry of crime.
These things I ask of you.
If you see it fit to be so…
If you see it fit to be your will…
then have mercy upon my lost soul.
Amen.

L.O.S.

<u>Crutches</u>

Crutches needed to hold me up.
Crippled by misplaced trust
in Society's lust.
From out of the dust to learn.
In the event I fail and burn.
Remember me as the world
continuously turns.
Crutches cast aside.
In God's laws we abide.
With nowhere to hide
I stumble into a storm.
Torn form birth by the curse of scorn.
In my brain change aint new.
Untrue lies, alibis of a time untold.
Crutches needed to prevent the cold
from invading my shelter.

L.O.S.

VI. A Dolphins' Charm

By
Carlos Bellamy

Michelle was eighteen years old. Eighteen! Womanhood was finally here. But things had not gone as planned. She was on her way to college to continue her education. Her major was Political Science. Her intentions were to become either a politician or a lawyer. She wanted to do something to make a change. Her parents were proud of her, and they continuously told her so. She had been raised in a strict Christian household, where education was stressed as an important tool for survival. They would be disappointed and unable to pursue her plans of higher education.

As her thoughts wandered, Michelle smiled when they finally rested on Tim. Now Tim, he was her ideal man. He was sensitive, intelligent, and extremely understanding. They had been sweethearts for the last four years. Their relationship had reached a level of maturity that surprised them both. Her smile soon faded as she reluctantly remembered how her tears had flowed, when Tim told her that he was leaving. Tim was a dancer with Hollywood dreams. And it just so happened that an agency in California had offered him the opportunity of a lifetime. Tim had been dancing ballet for the last eight years of his life. He was more than just good. He was exceptional. He said that dancing came natural to him. Ballet was his first love. She was his second.

Michelle's thoughts stopped wandering as she tried to focus on how she would break the bad news to her parents. She knew her parents would be dismayed without the prospect of future wedding bells. After four years of schooling, her parents had made it clear that it would be appropriate for her and Tim to get married. But the dismal news of Tim's departure would quickly disappear when the news of her pregnancy invaded their Christian minds.

Such an immature mistake not only put her future in a bracket of uncertainty, but it compromised the sacrifices her parents had made on her behalf. Not only would they be infuriated, they would be deeply disturbed.

Michelle was in tears. She had delivered the news to her parents and they reacted just as she predicted they would. She was now being lectured on the inadequate woes of teenage pregnancy. They made certain she knew that abortion was not an option to be even remotely considered. Responsibility was a virtue unseen, but felt and carried out in the hearts of every wholesome Christian family. Fornication was a plague cast upon the deeds of the saints. A horrific reminder that the flesh was weak and not to be trusted. Rather the spirit should be nurtured daily. Which in turn, builds a Godly foundation of morality whereupon holy principles are guides to a more prolific life.

After nine months of lectures on spiritual guidance, Michelle had a baby girl. She had already decided that she could not keep the baby. To raise a child at this stage would be detrimental to her dreams. She would have to give the child up. Her parents stubbornly refused to support an act of blatant fornication. They told her since she could not abide by their rules, once the baby arrived she had to leave. The only option they left her with was adoption.

....

Michelle's mind raced as she stood in front of the adoption agency. She had called earlier to make an appointment. She found the place in the yellow pages. The agency was named 'The House of Healing'. She was instructed to bring her child. They assured her the baby would receive the best of care. Not only was it an adoption agency, but it was also a foster home.

Michelle stood with Tina Mitchell in her arms. Tina! She had already named the child. It was the least she could do. The baby was calm as if though she completely trusted her mother. Tina looked as if though she was being held by angelic arms. Placed upon both of their necks was a gold necklace with a dolphin charm. The significance of the dolphin was that the dolphin was considered as a protector. It was Michelle's way of telling Tina that no matter what happened, she will always be there to protect her.

Michelle stared at the humongous stone building that was before her. It was a block long with a black iron gate surrounding it. She couldn't tell whether the gate was to ward off intruders or whether it was constructed for the purpose of keeping inhabitants within. The building was a dark-gray with a gothic look. The windows were oval with an abstract paint covering them. To Michelle they seemed like eyes. Not the kind that cried, they were more like the ones that silently stared and penetrated the forbidden locked doors that hid the secrets to your soul.

Michelle shivered as she walked past the black iron gate. She walked up a short flight of stairs and stopped at the building's entrance. Above the doors engraved into the stone was a slogan. It read, "Hollow hearts are not known to hold anything. The illusions that they are allowed to grasp are phantoms without even the slightest hint of life." Michelle had no idea what the slogan meant. She never stopped to consider why would an adoption agency have such a slogan. Determined to do what she came here to do, she entered the building.

Michelle quickly left the building. She got in her car and headed towards the airport. She had a plane to catch. She was off to Louisiana to continue her education. As she drove her mind wandered back to 'The House of Healing'. She had been introduced to a Mrs. Wright. Mrs. Wright ran both the adoption agency and the foster home. After going over the technicalities of protocol and procedure, Michelle explained the significance of the necklace that was around her and Tina's neck. She refused to leave until Mrs. Wright had promised her that when Tina reached an age where she could understand, the significance of the necklace would be explained to her.

Michelle reached the airport. As she exited her car, she was in tears. She cried for the tribulations and struggles she had faced so far in her short lifespan. But most of all, her tears were for her daughter Tina. Little helpless Tina who's mother had abandoned her. She grabbed her bags from the back seat and made her way to the airport terminal. She felt guilty for putting her dreams above the welfare of her own child. But she found assurance in the promise that was made to her. She truly believed Mrs. Wright would keep her promise. Michelle gently kissed the dolphin that was on her neck as she boarded the plane.

....

Tina put on her sunglasses inorder to block out the glare from the sun. It was August and Chicago was known for having hot summers. She stood on the DuSable Museum's historical steps. She had spent the last four years getting her priorities together. With the help of one of the founders of the prestigious Museum, Tina had been able to overcome many tribulations.

In less than two weeks she was scheduled to attend Grambling State University. Just six years ago, to her such a fate would have seemed impossible. Tina had been in and out of 'The House of Healing'. They had continuously attempted to place her in an abode with loving parents. But every since Trina had been made privy to the significance of the dolphin that she wore around her neck, she refused to be subjected to any household other than her biological mother's.

So at the age of ten, that was when she discovered the truth, Tina had decided to embark on a passionate journey to find her Mother. While deemed noble by some, her passion was considered rebellious and insolent to 'The House of Healing'. They responded with discipline. Tina's passion soon gave way to misplaced anger. Before she knew it, her life had led her down a road filled with mischief, mayhem, and misery.

Standing on the steps of the DuSable Museum, Tina silently reminisced on her four years at the Museum and how transitional they were to her life. She had learned a lot about African-American history. If ever asked, she would be able to inform whoever that Jean Baptiste' Pointe DuSable was the first Chicago citizen. She would also be able to tell them that, in 1915 a conference was held in Chicago initiating a black history movement. Led by Carter G. Woodson, the black community responded with the assistance of "key intellectuals and cultural leaders". The knowledge she cherished the most was that she knew the heart of Linda. The Museum was founded in 1961 with Linda's help. It was also with the help of Linda that Tina was able to turn her life around. Tina owed everything to Linda and the staff of DuSable Museum for encouraging her and for just being there when it seemed no one cared. She had not given up the search for her beloved Mother. She had just redefined her passions without allowing her desires to rule her life.

As Tina left the Museum, tears rolled down her eyes. She didn't want to look behind her. It would hurt too much. She headed back to her apartment and packed her meager possessions. She was on her way to Louisiana.

Louisiana wasn't what she had expected it to be. She had stereotyped the place as being country and out of style. But much to her surprise Louisiana was intriguingly different. They had a style of their own. It appealed to her and she soon blended in.

Tina was attracted to Grambling State University because it was deeply respected as a prestigious black university. Known to most as "the Cradle of the PRO's:" for being "PROlific, PROficient, PROductive, PROmoting, PROviding, and PROving", Tina had decided it was the right school for her.

Tina chose to major in Sociology. Taking her own personal experience as an example of disparity, she had decided to venture off into the field of sociology and show exactly how her environment had molded her character. She also desired to prevent the same from happening to other children who underwent similar tribulations.

Her Sociology teacher's name was Mrs. Brown. Tina liked her because she was a no nonsense woman who stressed the value of morals and virtues. Mrs. Brown looked as if though she was in her late twenties. She wore no make up. She didn't have any jewelry except for a necklace that she kept tucked in her blouse. As class was being dismissed, Mrs. Brown gave an assignment to write a poem about something significant.

....

Hard work had brought success along with many things. Marriage was one but happiness was not amongst them. Michelle knew the origins of her discontented feelings. Her maternal concerns went out to Tina, the daughter she gave up for adoption. Michelle had tried getting Tina's information form the adoption agency, but she was informed that it was not the practice of 'The House of Healing' to release any information pertaining to the whereabouts of children who had been abandoned by their parents. Michelle had been furious!!! She went to sleep thinking about her precious Tina. Little helpless Tina.

....

Tina dreamed she was back in the adoption agency. Her necklace fell out of her shirt and onto the floor. Somebody kicked it down the stairs. Panicking, Tina ran down the stairs inorder to retrieve her precious necklace. When she got down the stairs the necklace was gone. No dolphin, no mother. Tina started crying. Everybody was laughing at her. No dolphin, no mother. No dolphin, no mother. Startled by the nightmare, Tina woke up in tears. She drank a glass of water then returned to sleep.

....

The next day in class, Tina was the last one to read her poem.

Carlos Bellamy

A Journey

Today I start a journey.
Actually it's a continuation of past travels.
To search for a part of me, I never knew.
A part of me that I've always held close.
Dearest Mother, at times you're like a ghost.
Unseen. Nothing more than an illusion.
A mirage to my lonely eye.
A dry riverbed filled with dolphins.
The protector of hope. Faith reinstated.
At night when I close my eyes
together we roam through
the corridors of my heart.
When I awake I'm no longer alone.
Your love surrounds me with strength.
Charmed because you are with me.
Your courage encircles me with vigor.
Charmed because you are with me.
Your passion encompasses me with all that you are.
Charmed because you are with me.
Although past tears have been shed
in our future years, today's fears
will no longer exist for us.
Dearest Mother, I've come to understand.
Today I complete a journey.
Actually it's a continuation of the past.

L.O.S.

After Tina read her poem the class was dismissed. Before she could leave Mrs. Brown asked Tina if she could see Tina's Poem. As Tina handed the poem to Mrs. Brown the paper fell. They both reached down to grab it and bumped each other's heads. The necklaces that were around their necks fell out. A dolphin was on the end of both necklaces.

After a long pause, Mrs. Brown handed Tina a piece of paper off her desk. It was a poem.

T.I.N.A

Today **I** Need Affinity.
Tomorrow **I'll** Need Affection.
Today **I** Need Assurance.
Tomorrow **I'll** Need Acceptance.
Today **I** Need Absolution.
Tomorrow **I'll** Need Afflatus.

L.O.S.

After reading the poem, Tina pointed at the necklace that was on Michelle's neck. "Let me rub that."

Michelle looked at her strangely. "What did you say?"

"I said let me rub that."

"What do you mean? Let you rub what?"

"The necklace around your neck I would like to have it in my possession."

"Well why didn't you just say that?"

"I did. Let me rub that." Tina smiled, explaining to her mother that after switching necklaces, if they were ever separated again they would always have a momento of each other.

Michelle gave Tina her necklace. After caressing it for a brief moment, Michelle smiled as she put on the necklace that Tina gave her. She stepped towards Tina and told her in her most gentle voice that she loved her with all her heart. Tina hugged her mother and told her that she loved her just as much, if not more.

They stared at each other for what seemed like hours. What was once thought never to be had finally occurred. They held one another in a warm embrace and wept together. But instead of the usual sorrow that had once filled their hearts, their tears were now tears of joy. They were happy to be re-united. Happy to face whatever adversity tomorrow brought, as long as they remained together.

THE END

Carlos Bellamy

DICHOTOMY

Contents

Carlos Bellamy

Prologue

Dichotomy is the division or the process of dividing into, two especially mutually exclusive or contradictory groups. As defined by 'The Merriam-Webster Dictionary'. The division or the duality, that is expressed in this book is the one between Pain and Love. Both are experiences that we deal with throughout life. Whether the pain is physical, spiritual, or mental; we often find ourselves constantly seeking love, inorder to fill a dark and dreary void. Hopefully, this book will castrate the pain and suffering we fill, by offering love as a tool of healing.

Carlos Bellamy

I. <u>Pain</u>

"It is so seldom that a friendly voice reaches me. I am now alone, absurdly alone...and for years no refreshment, not a drop of humanness, not a breath of love has reached me."

Nietzsche

"There is no revenge like oblivion, for it is the entombment of the unworthy in the dust of their own nothingness."

Baltasar Gracian

Carlos Bellamy

The Hands Of Thieves
the sonnet of despair

Oh, Heavens! By what means do you grant me ink
only to have it stole by the hands of thieves?
The stench of treachery is a familiar stink
and it causes by my heart to be grieved.
I now know why the caged bird sings.
It is not what you call a song.
It is a lamentation of sorrow and quarantine.
A morbid tale that tells of sufferings and wrongs.
My pain refuses to give me his name.
I sit silent, revenge invades my mind.
It whispers tales that are both pleasant and strange.
He speaks of justice in due time.
If my heart and hand is to be defiled by men
then I will cut them off and never write again!

L.O.S.

Let Come, Whatever May
Written in hopes of a better tomorrow.

The walls whisper
but the language is undecipherable
to Society's sane minds.
Linguistic scholars, baffled beyond repair.
A stampede of echoes
silhouettes of a time once thought of.
Lost memories. Lets label them precious.
Grip them!! Not with our hands
but with medieval manacles.
To release them is to become
exactly what we are today.
To release them is for them
to never have been found.
Lost memories. Label them precious.
Once stained by the insane pain
of reform.
Let us nurture them.
Breast-fed thoughts of times
before the conditioning of similac.
Let come, whatever may.
Behold! Here comes a unicorn.
Mythical in more than one way.
The beauty of an illusion.
The grotesque glance of reality.
Clear-cut plans to erase love.
Muddy waters that blurs visions.
In contradiction to life.
Against the definitions
of the pursuit of happiness.
What would Thomas say?
He would probably cry
if he even remotely viewed
the lie, in which we live.
As if though words
the composition of the constitution
was nothing more than ornaments.
Decorations for the holidays.

163

Arrogant! Boldly placed upon our doors.
Destined to be taken down
and forgotten with the passing of the season.
Celebrations of hate.
Misery no longer feels
the touch of loneliness.
Let come, whatever may.
On this dark and cloudy night
as I defy Society with all my might
I desperately hope the choked throats
will stop to breathe.
We can't let corruption continue to succeed.
Let come, whatever may.
Is knowledge to be hoarded?
A gem shared with a chosen few?
A holy grail, searched for
found, but never mentioned?
Do not the common man count!?!?
I speak of a winter yet to be seen.
I know of a summer
that if fought for it could arrive.
I talk of a year unforgotten.
I whisper of a promise
that's no longer discussed.
Let come, whatever may.

L.O.S.

<u>Words In My Mouth</u>
**dedicated to the lost souls
who never spoke up for themselves.**

This nation was built upon a nation
by a stolen nation for a new nation.
If I was to stand up
and die challenging that
which is incorrect
would you, the people of America
support me?
Or would you simply grieve for
my greatness, or the lack thereof.
A misguided soul that's what they
will probably label me.
Discontent with the misery of poverty.
Determined to expose that any peace
hoped for as a result of war
is an illusion.
If I was to stand up and die
would you, my peers and friends
support me?
Better yet, if you could put words
in my mouth
what would you have me say?
Would you have me talk of past times
in a tone so demented
with a desire to travel back
and become unattached to those souls
who, have been notoriously and brutally tormented.
Would you have me furious
with the passions of Huey?
Would you have me explode
shocking the world with the
violent truth, as if though
my lips were Malcom's?
Would you have me preach
a sermon of dreams?
The latest rendition to Martin.
Instilling hope into the souls

of the young?
Would you have me write
as if though I was Langston?
If you could put words in my mouth
what would you have me talk
in similies, with tears on my cheeks?
Voice choked from suppressed anger.
Finally able to express long-felt pain.
The horror of silence
is to never be heard.
Imagine a life lived
without uttering a single word.
So I would ask of you
that from now on when you speak
make sure your words count.
Use each word as if though
it was your last.
Say something. Give life meaning.
Speak up! Or else be without a tongue.
Forever silent.
Know one thing people of America
the hatred that exists amongst us
is not from the origins of racism.
It comes from the neglect of humanity.
So when I ask you, answer me.
If you could put words in my mouth
what would you have me say?

L.O.S.

A Language Of Tears
inspired by Eldridge Cleaver's
'Soul On Ice'

An onus of unfulfilled oaths.
An esoteric of latent love.
A language of tears
silently shed
disgustedly discussed and experienced.
The egress of an epoch.
The birth of beauty unseen.
An aborted soul.
I am the ghost of what
America refuses to be.
They label my pen 'Unicorn'
for it symbolizes purity and peace.
A myth hoped for
but frightfully envisioned.
My heart searches surreptitiously
for a concealed love.
Someone to understand me.
Someone who actually sees me.
Someone who wants to be understood.
Someone who wants to be seen.
My heart has been exposed.
I stand unclothed in front of you.
Naked and unashamed.
Love me.
Unhug me.
Hate me.
Erase me.
The cycles of death.
I am confined within the
realms of my mind.
At war with my own ego.
I ask of you
do not aid him in his battle
for he is putrid, vile, and despicable.
The epitome of Society's conditioning.
Partially humble

Carlos Bellamy

I stumble from hunger.
Bombarded and overwhelmed
by an enlightened sense of perception.
It is a ferment and stigma
possibly too much to be bared.
My health fades fast.
While my mind continuously excels.
Will I succumb to the strains of stress?
I remain driven
and I consistently speak in
a language of tears.

L.O.S.

<u>What Color Is Freedom?</u>

All this talk of racism and colors
makes me wonder
what color is freedom?
Am I to believe that a certain color
will determine if I'm to be free or not?
And if so, am I to be deceived
to perceive that this is equality?
What color is freedom?
Does freedom have a color?
Knowing America they will say
freedom is white skin
or green paper.
What color is freedom?
Let's say freedom did have a color.
Would you be so bold as to describe
an iridescent hue of complexity?
Freedom is the color
of a soul who has been transformed
from ignorance to enlightenment.
Freedom is the color
of a child who has learned to read.
Freedom is the color
of an old man on his death bed
unafraid and at peace with God.
Freedom is the color
of a prisoner whose body
has been captured
but his mind roams daily.
Freedom is the color
Of an invisible man
who has finally been
accepted by society.
If freedom is all these
colors and so much more
I ask you...
What color is freedom?

L.O.S.

The Heresy Of Hate

Far from home, when I heard
word on my own death.
Like I was suppose to be
crushed and vexed.
Hushed and hexed!
Out of luck
stuck, on my last breath.
They say the autopsy revealed
I had a disease, they call mentally ill.
Although lyrically skilled
my tongue eloquent and finally still.
After the fire, 3 days of chill.
Then my corpse was stolen
from its tomb and concealed.
Follow that with news of me
miraculously healed.
Christian Crusades to ensure
my lips are sealed.
Poisonous moves! Monks burning my notes.
Hanging with ropes
anyone whoever heard what I wrote.
Envision the choked throats.
A legion of ears
gives birth to fears of an antidote.
They call my accursed pen
'Unicorn', the beast of hope.
Don't let him tell his-story about me!
Listen to me tell you about me.
Since I'm viewed as uncovering Society's hypocrisy
the Media won't endorse me.
So turn off yo radios, T.V.'s
and things that entertain.
Allow something constructive
to invade your brains.
I edutain.
Educate in a place
where Society has entertained.
Since I'm pressed for time

I'll give you my version in 8 lines.
Hold on! Before you scream guilty
let me plead my cause.
I was persecuted like apostle Paul.
Incarcerated and destined to a hostile fall.
I walked with my head held high
when they said I should've crawled.
So they say I fought back
and that's what started it all.
I seen dreams of better things.
But I won't preach about dreams
rather, I incite action in men.
Give me the honor of 10.
9 who lived without the painz of sin.
I guarantee the noblest death
since Sitting Bull and his kin.
Political prisoners proves liberty's
been raped.
I'm afraid you're not suppose
to hear the things I state.
They have the audacity to label me
the messenger of truth
as the heresy of hate.

L.O.S.

The Loss

The loss of literary works
finds me grieved.
The rush of depression
like a heavy weight champion
who I am hard-pressed to fend off.
Barely able to withstand
the fierceness of his blows.
I feel like I have lost a child.
The pain claws at my heart
numbing all emotions.
I want to hurt those
who have hurt me.
But to do so would contradict
my principles.
From the inside
I am shredded, torn to pieces.
I must and will rebuild
the good that is left to hold on to.
I stand at the grave
of a soul kidnapped.
My flesh of my flesh
stolen, abducted, seized
by stolen hands.
I must bury him
not only in the grave
but also in my heart
and move on.

L.O.S.

<u>Death</u>

I challenged you many times.
In a stupor with drunkard courage
I called upon you and your mistress.
Fate, the ironic whore.
She came at my request
but refused to soothe my tormented soul.
Floating as only the herbs could do.
I searched for you
unsuccessfully.
You coward!!!
Show your face to this
imprudent warrior.
Would you deny me a glimpse
at your dark silhouette?
Your name brings fear
to the hearts of men.
I am advanced in my ways.
I no longer search for you.
Amused by my liquid courage
I sit and wait.
Accomplishing as much as I can
until you come
accompanied by your cruel mistress.
And snatch me from these realms
of confusion.

L.O.S.

<u>You Made A Difference</u>
to Huey

You were strong
when others were weak.
You stood tall
when others crawled in fear.
You opened your mouth
and spoke, filling hearts
with courage and determination.
You climbed the steps
of injustice, searching for liberty.
You turned around to ensure
others that they too could climb.
You was pushed in the back.
And you fell down the steps
of injustice
landing in the dirts of despair.
Although we will not forget your fall.
The memories we cherish
are the ones where
you stood tall.
Huey, you made a difference
and we love you for that.

L.O.S.

A Thousand Times
the hurt continues

A thousand times I have died.
It seems no one wants to bury me.
A thousand times I have cried.
What is it that worries me?

I know of an epoch lost to my soul.
If I had to be born, why not there
where I could have been consoled?
Who would even venture to care?

A thousand times I have fought.
Win, lose, or tie.
A thousand times I have lossed
And been left stranded to die.

I never had the chance to choose
If given the news of hurt on Earth
I would have asked to wear aborted shoes
and returned to the comforts of the dirt.

A thousand times I have died.
It seems no one wants to bury me.
A thousand times I have cried.
What is it that worries me?

L.O.S.

Have Me

Oh, America!
Land of the unfree
and home of diaphanous documents.
How would you have me?
Probably with silent lips and a still heart.
Would you have me like Petrarch?
Filled with envy and attached to a lost love.
Would you have me like Dante?
Exiled from my own nation.
A self-proclaimed saint obsessed with fame.
Would you have me as Machiavelli?
Maliciously addicted to power
and the gaining thereof.
Would you have me like Martin?
Preaching dreams while being beaten with clubs.
Would you have me like Huey?
A fallen star abused by synthetic highs.
Would you have me like the Titan Goliath?
A fierce warrior whose invincibility was his demise.
How would you have me?
Let me tell you how I would have me.
I would have me humble.
Turning neither to the left
or right
in my quest for truth.

L.O.S.

<u>On An Island</u>
**Inspired by thoughts
of self-discipline.**

On an island, willingly
deserted by Society
with no one to talk to.
Conversations held
with shadows of a human being.
The discipline of self
gives birth to
the virtues of silence.
Nightmares of companionship.
Leave me to myself.
I need no politics.
I desire no government.
Loneliness is a thing unknown.
Insanity kept at bay
with the beauty of ink.
Expressions of self.
On an island, by choice.
Content with what is.
No longer hating what once was.
Happy thoughts are here.
My only condition
somebody please,
read what I have written.

L.O.S.

<u>Out Of The Mouth Of Madness</u>

What has happened to my humble heart?
I was a patriot from the start.
I've been removed so far apart
that they liken my nature to a shark.
Lusting for prey with a carnivorous tooth.
But I dare to declare
with a challenging air
that I am living proof
that our reality is stained
by the pains of altered truth.
Hold the fire of the assassins on the roof!
James Earl Ray, you go ahead and shoot.
They label me unfit to talk.
Confined in a cell
with limited space to walk.
Only time will tell
if the fate of all is to be outlined in chalk.
Listen to the call of the wild.
I will stand awhile on the wild
borderlines of insanity.
Where those who try to understand me
are doomed to fall over.
A somber sober soldier.
Footprints in the sand
not mine but Jehovah's.
Out of the mouth of madness
comes a scream of pain.
I am ashamed that I was once to blame
for ignorant acts, the tracks of the trained.
Out of the mouth of madness
comes a hysterical laugh.
The hurt is deep
and that is only the half.
The reason for our laughs
is that we don't want to be seen crying.
I live every day continuously dying.
I want to love you America.
But you have sinned against me America.

Out of your mouth the rhetorics of a hypocrite.
Speaking of Liberty, while swinging
wide-eyed with a blind fist.
I am madness, and out of my mouth comes words.
Nouns and verbs.
They are not words of hate.
But rather, words of love.
Out of the mouth of madness
who would expect such a thing?

L.O.S.

Carlos Bellamy

__Bitterness And The River__
**words only have power
if you allow them to.**

Save your bitter remarks
for a river
that doesn't flow.
A river that doesn't
flow can be filled
with bitterness
because it have
no outlets.
A flower river
continuously cleans itself
of unwanted things.

L.O.S.

<u>More</u>

More of life.
More of love.
More of joy.
More of reward.
More of materials.
More of something.
More of this.
More of that.
Just plain ol more.
Never really appreciating
what you already have.

L.O.S.

Carlos Bellamy

The Other Side

The grass always
looks greener
on the other side.
But an irrevocable
price is paid
once you jump
over the fence.

L.O.S.

<u>The Night</u>

the frightening whisperings of walls
the idea of creepy things that crawls

the fact of no light
the adjustment of sight

the notions of devils and demons
the joys or sometimes the horror of dreaming

the escape from daily routine
the night is a wonderful thing

L.O.S.

Carlos Bellamy

<u>I Aint Kilt Nobody</u>

I aint kilt nobody
but I still went to jail.
I aint kilt nobody
but they gave me life
to do in earthly hell.
I aint kilt nobody
my finga didn't pull da trigga man.
I aint kilt nobody
neither did anybody with me man.
I aint kilt nobody
so I'm spose ta be held accountable
for the actions of da unaccountable?
Don't make much sense ta me.
Not less you wanna RID da streetz
of roaches and things of da such.
Anyway yal put it
I aint kilt nobody!

L.O.S.

If The South Would've Won

If the South would've won
the Confederate flag would
probably still fly high.
Bigotry would still roam
the black roads of Mississippi
or Alabama.
If the South would've won
strange fruit
would be in the minds of all.
The Klan would probably
be infamously loved, hated
and well known.
If the South would've won
things would probably
be exactly as they are
TODAY.
After they couldn't
work the slaves anymore
they probably would've
threw them all in jail.
Or found some way for them
to kill each other.
Imagine that.

L.O.S.

If I Die...A Thugz Prayer
This is dedicated to my love ones
the ones who really care.
At my funeral recite this prayer
and my soul will listen as my body lies there.

If I die...if I die, don't cry
be brave and bury me paid.
For I have paid my dues
to this treacherous system.
Enchanted by the streets
I quickly became a victim.
I was robbed. My conscience
my morals, and my values were stole.
A so-called thug, I'm on bending knees
praying God restores my soul.
Death is near.
I can see it, but why release a tear?
I feel no fear.
I only hope I die in my sleep.
Maybe then my heart can find peace
and be relieved of its grief.
Eternal happiness is all I have ever desired.
If I die, don't cry...
pray I avoid Hell's fire.

NUTTIN NICE
THE GHETTO POET
L.O.S.

186

II. <u>Love</u>

"And why does it make you sad to see how everything hangs by such thin and whimsical threads? Because you're a dreamer, and incredible dreamer, with a tiny spark hidden somewhere inside you which cannot die, which even you cannot kill or quench and which tortures you horribly because all the odds are against its continual burning. In the midst of the foulest decay and putrid savagery, this spark speaks to you of beauty, of human warmth and kindness, of goodness, of greatness, of heroism, of martydom, and it speaks to you of love."

Eldridge Cleaver

After The Rain
the sonnet of hope

After the rain is finished
the sun shines down from up high.
Although it seems the pain is diminished
we never forget our reason 2 cry.
Yesterday's frowns, finally gone.
Replaced by high hopes and affectionate smiles.
Today we head for home
no longer burdened with yesterday's trials.
After the rain, the wind blows bringing change.
Who knows the direction Fate will travel?
Leave no trace, wash away the dirt and shame.
Let us bury the hurt from Hate, under the gravel.
The passionate promise of rainbows, eloquently spoke.
Follow my toes, as we embrace the ethos of hope.

L.O.S.

And What Do We Say

I see the painz of the past
in your eyes
and yet for some reason I smile.
I am assured.
I hear the misery of yesterday
in your voice
and yet for some reason I laugh.
I am assured.
I listen to the promise
of tomorrow as only you
can declare.
And yet for some reason I cry.
My soul has been fermented.
You whisper bold words of
encouragement in my ear.
Urging me to lift my head.
When I can bare to breathe no more
it is you that holds my heart
in your humble hand
with a gentle grip
and speak to me words
of life and love.
You speak similar words
to those heard
before man knew of language.
At times you are cold.
Elusive and seductive.
The mistress of want.
Seduced, I travel the corridors
of my cell.
In your name
I continue on.
You are in the hearts of all men.
I knew you as a child.
You kept the abusing hands
of poverty
from tearing my soul to pieces.
You are in the bosom of all women.

Carlos Bellamy

I saw you as a child.
You were a mother to me.
A grandmother.
You clothed me when I was naked.
You fed me when I was young.
A model in which to follow.
When times are at their worse
you are the first to come.
You have yet to leave.
Immortal.
That is what you are.
If not for you
I could not exist.
How do I repay you?
This poem could never
do you justice.
At last, my pen has failed me.
And what do we say…
…of Hope?

L.O.S.

Confessions Of An Unknown Love
a dream of mine

We're standing in what looks
like an alley with a group of people.
Everybody is incarcerated but you.
A truck drives pass and something
falls off of it.
(The truck is driven by a mechanic, like the ones who came and fixed the
big oven on Thanksgiving)
Just what I don't recall.
You turn towards us and asked
how did whatever fall, fall.
We didn't respond.
I knew why it fell
but I failed to respond.
You jump onto the back
of the truck.
(It looked liked the carts we take to transportation, but with a motor attached
to a front compartment. You know, like a pick-up truck, except the pick-up
part was the transportation cart.)
Possibly for a joy ride, I think.
I follow your lead.
After all, you are the affection
of my idea of love.
The truck drives into
a lake of water.
That was why the thing
that fell, fell off.
You move towards the front
of the truck.
I have just jumped on so
I am at the rear.
The speed of the truck
suddenly accelerates,
You are now in my arms
and we both fall into the water.
You laugh, claiming that
we tricked you.
It was a joke played on you

on our part.
At least, that's what you think.
The guys in the alley
they laugh with you.
They are laughing at the fact
that we fell.
It was not a joke
and I am not laughing.
I am sinking, headed underwater.
I am still holding on to you.
I look into your face and see
nothing but beauty.
We are submerged.
Your face is as calm as ever.
Your beauty intensifies.
Your expression reads that
you know how to swim
and it asks what about me.
My expression does not answer you.
I began to think that in highschool
I was on the swim team.
I used to be a lifeguard.
I've saved lives before.
Your expression remains calm.
You know how to swim
and I know you know how.
(Just exactly how I know I'm not sure. Maybe its your expression that tells
me. Anyway, I know with a certainty that you can swim. Can you swim?)
Your expression asks me
calmly can I swim.
We are steadily sinking.
My expression does not answer you.
(I Can't Imagine Why Not! The answer eludes me.)
My expression belies my
ability to swim.
I am misrepresented, misunderstood.
(by even me at times)
We are steadily sinking
and I realize this.
I began to panic and suddenly
I know how I will die.
I will drown.

(Without ever knowing your love. Or without me ever confessing my love
for you.
Although, I think you know how I feel.)
Your face is no longer calm.
Sinking.
I began to swallow water
thinking no longer of death
but all my thoughts become
a single thought of you.
To die in your arms.
Your love is forbidden to me.
But your sorrow will not be.
I am no longer holding you.
You are now holding me.
You desperately, swim for the surface.
Trying to save my life.
But I am not helping you.
I wish to die in your arms
can't you see that?
If I have your sorrow
I will forever be a part of your heart.
You try harder to save me.
But if you fail to save me
then I succeed in becoming a part
of your heart.
If you save me then I fail.
I cannot afford such misery.
I express nothing to you.
My face belies my calm.
It still reads as if I am
panicking and wants to be saved.
You are more determined than
ever to save me.
You began to make progress.
We are headed to the surface.
Disgusted, I break away from you.
How could you do this to me?
You are the affection of my
idea of love.
I am in love with the
idea of love
and that idea has become you.

You inspired me to write a poem
entitled 'Only Lord Knows Why'.
I showed that to you.
(How I found the courage to do so, I don't know.)
You also inspired me to write two
more poems. 'Unspoken Heart'
and 'I See Pieces Of Me In You'.
I never found the courage to show
you the last two.
And now you inspire me to compose this.
(I will call it 'Confessions Of A Unseen Love'. The pleasure in writin this
is that once you read it you will know everything.)
I break away from you.
You look confused, but just as
beautiful as ever.
(I remember talking to someone. You happen to walk pass and I wanted a
woman's
perspective on the issue. We were discussing my mother. I asked you to
come here, for a second. You walked over to where we was. And it just so
happens that it was the closest we ever been face to face. Our faces was
inches apart, but it was completely innocent. I remember being literally
struck to silence by your beauty. Imagine me, a poet, loss for words! I
inhaled sharply and marveled the reflection of a Goddess in my very
presence. In those few seconds, I lived a lifetime.)
I am sinking once more.
I would rather die than
to live without a part of me
in your heart.
You looked confused, but just as
beautiful as ever.
You stop swimming.
I think you are about
to come down to where I am
and try to save me again.
Maybe you need to.
I read this in your expression
and I flee.
I will not give you the
honor of saving me.
I will save myself.
I began to swim at an angle.
Far away from you as possible.

But I am headed for the surface.
You continue swimming up
now assured that I'm safe.
I began to panic.
Thinking I'll never make it.
We have been under the water
far too long.
In my foolishness I swam
at an angle, when I should
have shot straight up.
(I wanted to get away from you.)
I visualize us both hitting
the surface at the same time.
I now know with a certainty
that I will not make the surface.
I now want to live.
Worse than ever before.
I can feel it in my heart.
Where are you!?!?
Why don't you save me?
Frantically I swim for the surface.
(It hurts to recall this)
There's nothing but water.
Water above me.
Water around me.
Water underneath me.
The water is beautiful.
Possibly more beautiful than you.
I never make the surface.
I wake out of my sleep
(or did the dream switch to something else?)
before I actually drown.
And yet, somehow
it was one of the best dreams
I ever had.

L.O.S.

<u>Someone Special</u>
written after watching 'Felicity'
thinking of someone in particular

I just wanna be loved.
To be held.
To be touched.
For my heart to be caressed
by another soul.
I want someone to love.
Someone to adore.
Someone to understand
who understands me.
I have walked the shores
of many oceans.
Soaking my feet in puddles
of tears.
For years, I have existed
without the embrace of love.
Maybe the ocean is proof
that Jesus saw my pain
and wept for me.
I want someone to whisper to.
Someone to hug.
To hold hands, knowing that
even time couldn't separate
the bonds of our affinity.
I would like to wake up
and be ensured by confidence
that my heart could know
no other love.
I want someone to kiss
in the morning.
You know, before
you brush your teeth.
I no longer search for security.
I no longer search for comfort.
I need not search for passion.
She is kin to my heart.
Everytime we communicate

Everytime we converse in discourse
I wonder...
I pray...
I hope...
I wish...
I long for you to see
that it is possible
for you to become everything
I have mentioned
and so much more.
You're special.

L.O.S.

Beauty

Beauty is perceived
with the eyes of reality.
A pleasure to the senses
it is just what it is.
Not what it ought to be.
It is what everything is.
A beauty unseen
anticipating the oohs & aahs.
Appreciating the warmth
derived from multiple hearts.
Beauty is...
the hues of a rainbow
the birth of a newborn
the smile of companionship
the glimpse of a sunrise
glowing skies, ablazed.
Mountains crested with snow.
A culture remembered
embraced lovingly by
loving descendants.
A green forest
filled with wild-life
uninvaded by the pollution
of industrial revolutions.
Beauty is love
which in its highest element
is a principle
to the roads of truth.

L.O.S.

<u>Unequal Love</u>
My name is Dorothy.
This is written to Paco.

Your love for me had no limits.
You were a sweet and loving guy.
I cared for you
but not as much as you did for me.
Out of your respect for me
you refused to dishonor me in God's eyes.
Celibate relations of a love
sent down by the Heavens.
But I was naïve.
My carnal desires were insatiable.
I betrayed your trust.
It was simply the whisperings of lust.
You found out and asked questions.
I told you I had been seeing
someone for awhile.
I told you one had to be cut loose.
You looked at me with your
heart's eye.
Asking not to be the one to go.
As much as it hurt me to say so
I released our love.
Your tears only made things worse.
I gave you a sponge to wipe your eyes.
Comforted you in my own way.
Three weeks later, I called you.
I made a mistake.
Realizing that I requested
a second chance.
Would I get to see your love?
You forgave me.
Eventhough I didn't deserve
to be forgave.
Our love intensified.
My love finally the equal of yours.
Joe is a sign of that.
Flesh of my flesh.
Blood of your blood.

Our love magnified.
My love finally the equal of yours.
Ronnie is a sign of that.
Flesh of your flesh.
Blood of my blood.
We're soon to be married.
Saturday.
Friday we made the best love ever.
My heart is eternally yours.
I love you.
And I know you love me.
What's understood
need not be said.
Saturday has come.
Where are you my love?
Invitations have been sent.
Everyone has come to see
us united as one.
Our love was sent down
by the Heavens!
Or was it?
Hold on!!! Did you really
forgive me?
Or was the second chance
a filthy lie?
I am a tortured soul.
I stare out the window
of my cell
I am a patient.
They say I'm mentally ill.
How I got here I knoweth not.
All I know is that
love is unequal.
Never again will I love.

L.O.S.

Tomorrow's Song

I'm tired of singing
sad songs.
Today I talk of
roses and dandelions.
Blue skies.
Rivers filled with fish.

L.O.S.

Carlos Bellamy

Optimism

And what of optimism?
That brave young soldier
with high hopes
who once held
his head high.
I hear he is now
a crippled veteran
and even more determined
than before.
What of him?

L.O.S.

<u>Life</u>

What could I possibly
say about you?
The essence of all.
Intrinsic to existence.
You are unprejudiced
bestowing your gift on all.

L.O.S.

Carlos Bellamy

<u>Say Something</u>

Hey! Why don't somebody
say something?
Yeah, I hear yal talking
but say something.
Something that means
something.
Something that counts.
Why all the sad faces
and songs of sorrow?
Yal gone stop living
just cuz yal locked up?
Don't make no sense.

L.O.S.

Acknowledgements

I thank the following for their patience and dedication to the publishing of this book:

1. Howard Harris Jr.
2. Ronald A. West
3. Michael Bellamy
4. Evette M. Scott
5. Anthony Bellamy
6. Nicholas Medina
7. Bryan Powers
8. Henry Morris
9. Juanita Dale
10. Tommy Hanes
11. Tony DuSuno
12. Percy Fields
13. Terry Davis
14. John P. Bellamy
15. Arabella Fails
16. Crystal Powers
17. Roosevelt Lockhart
18. Rimbu Ellohim
19. Malcom Nelson
20. Stanetta Jackson
21. John Mosley
22. Stancle Foster
23. Wayne Strawder
24. Velda A. Kelley
25. DeAndre Powers
26. Tom Konerzer
27. Nate Unger
28. Mildred Manuel
29. Oscar Charles
30. Tammy M. Zaia
31. Felicia Hill
32. Levi Crawford
33. Tabas Jackson
34. Adrianne Powers
35. Gladys Dodson

36. Shaq Johnson
37. Lurena Stokes
38. Cherie Perry
39. Yvonne Perry
40. Carl A. Powers
41. Sharon A. Powers
42. Delores Bellamy
43. Lucius Bellamy
44. Larry Wade
45. Angela Wade
46. John Bellamy Jr.
47. Timothy Bellamy
48. Venus Mondie
49. Loletta Walker
50. Tony Ross
51. Mona Portis
52. Little Cool
53. Anthony Bunch
54. Porfirio C. Guttierez

About the Author

The author graduated from Hefferan grammar school, located on the Westside of Chicago, Illinois. He then attended and graduated from Whitney M. Young Magnet Highschool. After one year at Southern Illinois University at Carbondale, the author discovered his passion for writing. However, he contributes his enlightenment not to the formal miseducation of America's school system, but rather to the workings of self-education. In this respect, he is similar to Malcom X, who also became self-educated while serving time.

www.ingramcontent.com/pod-product-compliance
Lightning Source LLC
Chambersburg PA
CBHW030315290526
45785CB00001B/366